# How to Use This Book

## Look for these special features in this book:

SIDEBARS, CHARTS, GRAPHS, and original MAPS expand your understanding of what's being discussed—and also make useful sources for classroom reports.

FAQs answer common Frequently Asked Questions about people, places, and things.

WOW FACTORS offer "Who knew?" facts to keep you thinking.

TRAVEL GUIDE gives you tips on exploring the state—either in person or right from your chair!

PROJECT ROOM provides fun ideas for school assignments and incredible research projects. Plus, there's a guide to primary sources—what they are and how to cite them.

Please note: All statistics are as up-to-date as possible at the time of publication. Population data is taken from the 2010 census.

Consultants: Anna M. Cruse, Assistant Professor, School of Geology, Oklahoma State University; William Loren Katz; Steve Wilson, author of *Oklahoma Treasures* and *Treasure Tales*

Book production by The Design Lab

Library of Congress Cataloging-in-Publication Data
Orr, Tamra.
 Oklahoma / Tamra B. Orr. — Revised edition.
  pages cm. — (America, the beautiful. Third series)
 Includes bibliographical references and index.
 ISBN 978-0-531-24897-3 (lib. bdg.)
 1. Oklahoma—Juvenile literature. I. Title.
 F694.3.O77 2014
 976.6—dc23                                   2013033040

Revised Edition

AMERICA ★ THE ★ BEAUTIFUL

# Oklahoma

BY TAMRA B. ORR

Third Series, Revised Edition

Children's Press®
An Imprint of Scholastic Inc.
New York ★ Toronto ★ London ★ Auckland ★ Sydney
Mexico City ★ New Delhi ★ Hong Kong
Danbury, Connecticut

# CONTENTS

# GROWTH AND CHANGE

## 4

Newcomers race to claim land, Native Americans fight to keep the settlers out, and Oklahoma achieves statehood. . . . . . **38**

# MORE MODERN TIMES

## 5

Oil production changes everything, Oklahomans survive the Dust Bowl and other challenges, and a new century dawns. . . **52**

# TRAVEL GUIDE

## 9

Tour the scenic prairies, visit Native American museums, and experience the history of the West. . . . **104**

## PROJECT ROOM

★

COLORADO

KANSAS

Black Mesa

Selman
Bat Cave

Cimarron River

Cimarron

National
Wrestling Hall
of Fame and
Museum

Arkansas River

Arkansas

Ozark
Mountains

Plains Indians
and Pioneers
Museum

WOODWARD

ENID

TULSA

TAHLEQU

ROUTE 66

Oklahoma
Route 66
Museum

International
Rodeo
Finals

OKLAHOMA

Cherokee
Heritage
Center

OKLAHOMA CITY

Canadian

Tsa-La-Gi
Ancient
Village

Wichita Mountains
Wildlife Refuge

LAWTON

Red
River

MCALESTER

TEXAS

N
W        E
S

**QUICK FACTS**

**State capital:** Oklahoma City
**Largest city:** Oklahoma City
**Total area:** 69,898 square miles
(181,035 sq km)
**Highest point:** Black Mesa,
4,973 feet (1,516 m)
**Lowest point:** Little River,
289 feet (88m)

0                    60
Miles

# Welcome to Oklahoma!

## HOW DID OKLAHOMA GET ITS NAME?

In the Choctaw language, *ukla* means "people" and *huma* means "red." Allen Wright, the principal chief of the Choctaw Nation, went to Washington, D.C., as a negotiator during treaty discussions in 1866. While he was there, he came up with the name, which means "Territory of the Red People."

MISSOURI

ILLINOIS

INDIANA

KENTUCKY

TENNESSEE

ARKANSAS

ALABAMA

LOUISIANA

MISSISSIPPI

OKLAHOMA

8

# READ ABOUT

The Nature Conservancy's Tallgrass Prairie Preserve near Pawhuska

CHAPTER ONE

# LAND

★

IF YOU'VE NEVER SEEN OKLAHOMA, YOU MIGHT THINK THAT IT IS A DRY, DUSTY, FLAT STATE. But that is not true. There is a great deal of variety within its 69,898 square miles (181,035 square kilometers). Top to bottom—from the highest point at Black Mesa, at 4,973 feet (1,516 meters), to the lowest point on the Little River, at 289 feet (88 m)—Oklahoma is worth a closer look.

**Q: HOW BIG IS THE PANHANDLE?**

**A:** This area is 5,687 square miles (14,728 sq km), includes three counties, and is larger than the state of Connecticut.

## A UNIQUE SHAPE

Oklahoma is in the south-central United States, just north of Texas. It is bordered by six states: Texas, New Mexico, Colorado, Kansas, Missouri, and Arkansas. Perhaps what sets Oklahoma off more than anything else is its unique shape. The long, narrow strip in the northwestern part of Oklahoma reaches out and looks like the handle of a kitchen pot. It's no wonder the area is called the Panhandle. It measures 167 miles (269 km) in length and only 34 miles (55 km) in width.

Oklahoma lies in the Great Plains, and its elevation drops almost 3,000 feet (900 m) from west to east. The Red River runs along the state's southern border with Texas.

## PREHISTORIC BEGINNINGS

While Oklahoma is largely covered by vast prairies today, this was not always the case. Millions of years ago, the land that would one day become Oklahoma was completely covered in forests. It looked something like today's Vermont or Maine. Back then, the Rocky Mountains did not exist, so rain clouds that formed over the Pacific Ocean could travel all the way from the

The Cimarron River, which has a muddy, red color, flows through the Panhandle of Oklahoma.

west coast of North America to what is now Oklahoma. These clouds brought rain, which allowed the vast forests to grow.

Needlegrass and other grasses and flowers grow in the Tallgrass Prairie Preserve.

The Rocky Mountains formed between 35 million and 70 million years ago, slowly growing taller year by year. As they rose, they began to block the rain-filled clouds that rolled in from the Pacific. Rain would fall on the western side of the Rocky Mountains, leaving little for the eastern side. As Oklahoma became drier and drier, most of the vast forests eventually gave way to large swaths of prairie.

The major mountain ranges found in Oklahoma are the Ouachitas, the Arbuckles, and the Wichitas. The Ouachitas are in southeastern Oklahoma, the Arbuckles are in the central part of the state, and the Wichitas are

Turner Falls in the Arbuckle Mountains

located in the southwest. While these high areas are called mountains, many of the peaks rise to only about 1,500 feet (450 m). They are not as tall or as jagged as the Rocky Mountains, which have an average height of 10,000 feet (3,000 m). Oklahoma's mountains formed about 300 million years ago, making them much older than the Rockies. The Ouachitas, the Arbuckles, and the Wichitas were once as tall or taller than the Rockies are today. Over time, rain, wind, snow, and ice worked together to erode the mountains in Oklahoma to their present, relatively low height.

# Oklahoma Topography

Use the color-coded elevation chart to see on the map Oklahoma's high points (dark red to orange) and low points (green to dark green). Elevation is measured as the distance above or below sea level.

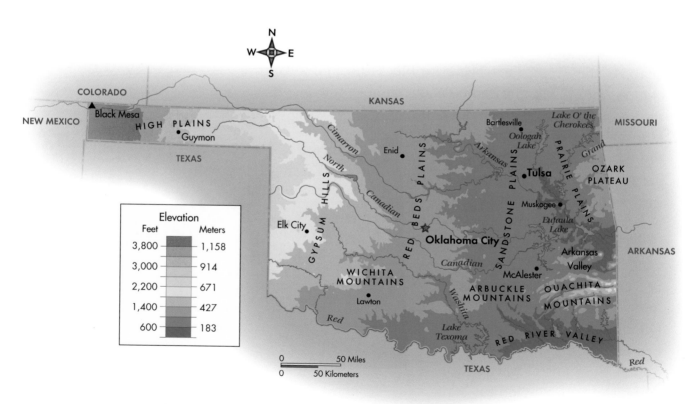

## LAND REGIONS

Oklahoma can be divided into ten geographical regions: the Ozark **Plateau**, Prairie Plains, Sandstone Hills, Ouachita Mountains, Arbuckle Mountains, Wichita Mountains, Red River Valley, Red Beds Plains, **Gypsum** Hills, and High Plains. Each region is quite distinct. The only thing the east and west sides of the state have in common is that they share the Red River.

### Ozark Plateau and Prairie Plains

The Ozark Plateau is found in northeastern Oklahoma. It continues into southern Missouri and northern Arkansas as well. This is a region of rolling hills created millions of years ago by the same forces that created the Ouachita and Arbuckle mountains. Since then, erosion has carved the land surface to create deep valleys with gently flowing streams and rivers.

The Prairie Plains region lies west and south of the Ozark Plateau. Much of the Prairie Plains area is used for farming and the raising of cattle.

**A scenic drive through the Ouachita National Forest**

## WORDS TO KNOW

**plateau** *an elevated part of the earth with steep slopes*

**gypsum** *a soft, white mineral*

### SEE IT HERE!

**MUSEUM OF THE RED RIVER**

In 1983, the complete fossilized skeleton of one of the rarest dinosaurs in the world was found in southeastern Oklahoma. It was an *Acrocanthosaurus atokensis*, a predator almost as big as the *Tyrannosaurus rex*. It took scientists three years to unearth it completely! The remains were very fragile, so molds of the fossilized bones were made and full skeletons were created for viewing. Today, a replica of that dinosaur's skeleton is on display at the Museum of the Red River in Idabel.

# Oklahoma Geo-Facts

Along with the state's geographical highlights, this chart ranks Oklahoma's land, water, and total area compared to all other states.

**Total area; rank** . . . . . 69,898 square miles (181,035 sq km); 20th
**Land; rank** . . . . . . . 68,667 square miles (177,847 sq km); 19th
**Water; rank** . . . . . . . . 1,231 square miles (3,188 sq km); 30th
**Inland water; rank** . . . 1,231 square miles (3,188 sq km); 17th
**Geographic center** . . . . . . 8 miles (13 km) north of Oklahoma City
**Latitude** . . . . . . . . . . . . . . . . . . . . . . . . . . . 33° 35′ N to 37° N
**Longitude** . . . . . . . . . . . . . . . . . . . . . . . 94° 29′ W to 103° W
**Highest point** . . . . . . . . . . . . . Black Mesa, 4,973 feet (1,516 m)
**Lowest point** . . . . . Little River, 289 feet (88 m), in McCurtain County
**Largest city** . . . . . . . . . . . . . . . . . . . . . . . . . . . Oklahoma City
**Longest river:** . . . Two great river systems run through Oklahoma, the Red River (which forms a boundary with Texas) and the Arkansas

Source: U.S. Census Bureau, 2010 census

Oklahoma is ranked 20th in size in the country. The state of Rhode Island would fit inside it almost 70 times!

## WORD TO KNOW

**bogs** *areas of wet, spongy ground*

## Sandstone Hills and Ouachita, Arbuckle, and Wichita Mountains

The Sandstone Hills extend south from the Kansas border to the Red River. The hills are 250 to 400 feet (75 to 120 m) high and are home to lush forests.

The Ouachita Mountains lie in the southeastern part of the state. The amount of rain that falls here is almost double what falls in the western part of the state, so the land is rich with streams, mineral springs, and waterfalls. It also has its share of **bogs** and cypress swamps.

The Arbuckle Mountains lie in south-central Oklahoma and they rise just 600 to 700 feet (180 to 210 m) above the plains. In the southwestern part of the state lie the Wichita Mountains.

## Red River Valley and Red Beds Plains

The Red River Valley is located along the Texas border and is marked by forested hills and rich soil.

The Red Beds Plains is the largest region in the state. It extends from the Kansas border in the north into the center of Oklahoma. The eastern part is forested, while the western part is covered with prairies.

## Gypsum Hills and High Plains

To the west of the Red Beds Plains are the Gypsum Hills. They reach in to the northwestern part of the

Parts of the Red River Valley and the Red Beds Plains are heavily forested.

state. This region is characterized by prairies and **mesas**. The soil here is bright red, a result of the iron oxide in it. This region has something different almost everywhere you turn. For example, there are canyons that were formed more than 200 million years ago. One spectacular sight is Alabaster Cavern. Its **buttes** are striped with the mineral gypsum, which sparkles in the afternoon sun.

The High Plains are in the northwestern part of the state. Seabirds soar over these salt plains, an area formed when the region was covered by water nearly 200 million years ago. In this region is the highest point in the state: Black Mesa.

## WATERWAYS

Oklahoma is a state with a lot of waterways—23,000 miles (37,000 km) of them, in fact. The Red River forms the southern border with Texas, while the Arkansas River enters the state in the northeastern corner. Oklahoma has more than 300 lakes, and most of them

### WORDS TO KNOW

**mesas** *flat-topped hills*

**buttes** *narrow, flat-topped hills with very steep sides; types of mesas*

A dam holds back the roaring Arkansas River.

## WORDS TO KNOW

**hydroelectric plants** *facilities that use water power, typically through a dam, to produce electricity*

**reservoir** *a lake or tank for storing water*

are human-made. They were created to help control flooding and to power **hydroelectric plants**.

Hydroelectric plants use water to produce power. They are often considered the best solution to a state's need for energy. These plants do not burn fuel, so there is no pollution like there is when burning resources such as coal and oil. No deep mines or wells have to be dug in order to construct a hydroelectric plant. The water itself is free. However, in the western United States it is often in short supply. On the downside, hydroelectric plants require huge amounts of money and land to build because they need a dam and a **reservoir**. Construction often results in the death of many different kinds of fish. Some are harmed by the plant's equipment. Others die when the water in their natural habitat is diverted.

## CLIMATE

One challenge the people of Oklahoma must deal with is the weather. One of the state's hardest times came more than 70 years ago. High winds blew through the state, causing a drought (an extended period without enough rainfall), which led to severe dust storms. The state became known as the Dust Bowl. Crops were ruined, and many people lost their jobs and incomes.

Masses of warm, moist air and cold, dry air often collide in the skies over Oklahoma. This creates conditions that cause tornadoes. Oklahoma lies in the heart of Tornado Alley, an area that extends across the middle of the country from Texas

## OKLAHOMA'S TWISTERS

| Year | Location | Casualties |
| --- | --- | --- |
| 1893 | Cleveland County | 31 dead, 100 injured |
| 1905 | Jackson County | 97 dead, 150 injured |
| 1920 | Cherokee County | 71 dead, 100 injured |
| 1930 | Oklahoma City | 23 dead, 125 injured |
| 1942 | Paden, Boley, Welty | 35 dead, 80 injured |
| 1945 | Pushmataha County | 69 dead, 353 injured |
| 1947 | Woodward | 113 dead, 900 injured |
| 1955 | Blackwell | 20 dead, 280 injured |
| 1960 | Wilburton | 16 dead, 106 injured |
| 1999 | Bridge Creek, Moore, Del City, and Oklahoma City | 38 dead, 800 injured |
| 2013 | Moore | 24 dead, 377 injured |

The spirits of the residents of Moore, Oklahoma, remained strong after the destructive tornado of May 20, 2013.

Per square mile, Oklahoma has more tornadoes and severe thunderstorms than any other state!

to South Dakota. Tornado winds can blow at 200 to 300 miles per hour (300 to 500 kph). These strong cyclones topple trees, down power lines, and destroy homes and sometimes entire communities. People must move to basements or other protected areas for safety.

May 3, 1999, marked the beginning of what is known as the Oklahoma Tornado Outbreak. This was a series of storms that lasted for three days and affected Oklahoma, Kansas, Tennessee, and Arkansas. Winds that hit Oklahoma City during this time were clocked at 318 miles per hour (512 kph), the highest tornado wind speed ever recorded on earth.

Thunderstorms are also common in Oklahoma. In the late spring and early summer, huge clouds can tower up to 70,000 feet (21,000 m) high. In fact, from April

A tornado crosses a highway in Beaver County. This storm roared over the plains in March 2007.

through July, the state experiences some of the most severe thunderstorms in the world. Large amounts of rainfall can cause lakes and rivers to rise. This often results in flooding, which can damage homes, businesses, and other structures.

Aside from these weather extremes, Oklahoma has a temperate, or mild, climate for most of the year. Summers can be hot, with temperatures frequently hitting triple digits. And some winter days can have temperatures below zero. The state gets snow each year, ranging from about 4 inches (10 centimeters) in the southern part of the state to about 20 inches (50 cm) near the Colorado border.

## PLANT LIFE

The fertile soil of Oklahoma nourishes a wide variety of flowers, plants, and trees. Because of its warm weather, the state has an unusually long growing season, averaging 238 days. Oklahoma is home to more than 130 types of trees, including mesquite, juniper, oak, hickory, pine, maple, cedar, cypress, and cottonwood. The redbud is Oklahoma's state tree. Colorful prairies glow with sagebrush, black-eyed susans, butterfly weed, and prai-

# Weather Report

**TEMPERATURE 120°F**

**TEMPERATURE -31°F**

This chart shows record temperatures (high and low) for the state, as well as average temperatures (July and January) and average annual precipitation.

**Record high temperature** . . . . . . . . . . . . . . 120°F (49°C) at Alva on July 18, 1936; at Altus on July 19 and August 12, 1936; and at Poteau on August 10, 1936

**Record low temperature** . . . . . . . . . . . . –31°F (–35°C) at Nowata on February 10, 2011

**Average July temperature, Oklahoma City** . . . . . . . . 83°F (28°C)
**Average January temperature, Oklahoma City** . . . . . . 39°F (4°C)
**Average annual precipitation, Oklahoma City** . . . . . 36.5 inches (92.7 cm)

Source: National Climatic Data Center, NESDIS, NOAA, U.S. Dept. of Commerce

Juniper tree

rie coneflowers. The official state plant is mistletoe. It was adopted in 1893, before Oklahoma was even a state. The state flower is the Indian blanket, a red flower with yellow-tipped petals. It can be seen along many of Oklahoma's roadways.

## ANIMAL LIFE

Oklahoma is rich in all kinds of animal life. Some of the most common animals are armadillos, coyotes, rabbits, mink, otters, foxes, and black bears. The state animal is the bison, or American buffalo. Bison are massive animals, weighing between 800 and 2,000 pounds (350 and 900 kilograms) and standing almost 6 feet (180 cm) tall at the shoulders. The animal was reintroduced into the Wichita Mountains Wildlife Refuge in 1907. Bison

## THE INDIAN BLANKET LEGEND

According to an old story, there was an Indian blanket maker who was known for miles around for his beautiful blankets. Everyone wanted one, and people would travel for hundreds of miles to trade for one. One day, he realized he was getting old, so he began weaving his own burial blanket. He included his favorite colors of brown, red, and yellow.

After the blanket maker died, his family wrapped him in the blanket, as the man's gift to the Great Spirit. The Great Spirit was pleased with the beauty of the blanket, but he was also sad. He knew that only those who had died would be able to look upon this beautiful creation. So he decided to give a gift back to the people still on earth.

The following spring, wildflowers of the same colors and design appeared on the blanket maker's grave. From there, they spread out across the land.

Bison

Mexican free-tailed bats take to the night sky in northwest Oklahoma.

## OKLAHOMA'S ENDANGERED SPECIES

What do the least tern, the red-cockaded woodpecker, and the whooping crane have in common? These birds are all endangered species in Oklahoma. That means these animals could die out if their habitats are not protected. Often the wetlands they rely on are destroyed when land is developed. Or, for the whooping crane, humans have disturbed their migratory routes. But Oklahomans are working to help protect these and other animals that make the state their home.

are now also found in the Tallgrass Prairie Preserve, a region managed by the Nature Conservancy.

Oklahoma's skies are often full of birds—from mockingbirds and orioles to meadowlarks, blue jays, and cardinals. The state bird is the scissor-tailed flycatcher. It has a long, forked tail that makes up more than half of its 14-inch (36 cm) length. The flycatcher is known for attacking any large bird that enters its nesting area. In the spring, they entertain many with their "sky dancing." To attract a mate, they swoop, twirl, and dive, using their long tails to keep their balance.

Stop by the town of Freedom any summer night and see the sky fill with a million Mexican free-tailed bats coming out of Selman Bat Cave. They are on their way to feast on moths, beetles, and other insects!

## EXPLORING THE LAND OF THE PRAIRIE GRASSES

One thing Oklahoma excels in is growing prairie grasses. While you may think that prairie grass is all one plant, there are really a number of different species, which vary in height, growing season, and water requirements. In the western part of the state, blue grama grass grows short, about 6 to 8 inches (15 to 20 cm) high. It is incredibly drought resistant. The grass is mixed with wildflowers, and bison and pronghorn wander through it to graze. Central Oklahoma has a vast mix of wheatgrass, needlegrass, and little bluestem, while the northwest has endless acres of strictly wheatgrass. In the east are the tallgrasses. There, the Indian grass, switchgrass, and big bluestem all grow as high as 8 feet (2.4 m). The Tallgrass Prairie Preserve is in this part of the state. It is a 37,000-acre (15,000-hectare) area filled not only with towering grasses but also with 79 species of mammals, 300 kinds of birds, and more than 500 species of plants.

## PROTECTING THE ENVIRONMENT

Oklahoma faces a number of important environmental issues today. One major concern is keeping the natural water resources clean. In 1992, the Oklahoma Water Resources Board (OWRB) created a program called Oklahoma Water Watch. This program encourages Oklahomans to participate in the protection and maintenance of the state's rivers and lakes. Volunteers learn about the importance of water resources and the methods used to monitor water quality. More than 500 volunteers have been certified through Oklahoma Water Watch, and hundreds of students from universities and public schools participate in the effort to keep Oklahoma's water clean and safe.

The Oklahoma Water Resources Board enlists the help of trained volunteers to monitor the quality of the state's water.

# Oklahoma National Park Areas

This map shows some of Oklahoma's national parks, monuments, preserves, and other areas protected by the National Park Service.

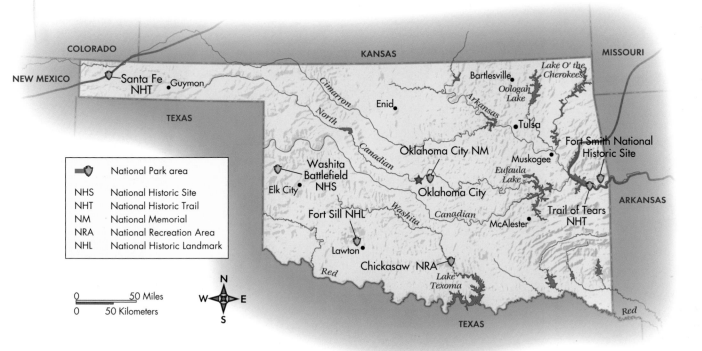

**Legend:**

|  |  |
| --- | --- |
| ⛨ | National Park area |
| NHS | National Historic Site |
| NHT | National Historic Trail |
| NM | National Memorial |
| NRA | National Recreation Area |
| NHL | National Historic Landmark |

An important member of the Oklahoma governor's executive branch is the secretary of the environment. The secretary's office works to protect and enhance the state's natural areas through conservation and education. It also enforces laws about pollution prevention and provides guidelines for maintaining water quality in the state.

Throughout Oklahoma, citizens are doing their part, too. For instance, the Metropolitan Environmental Trust in Tulsa encourages people to recycle, and has set up recycling centers throughout the Tulsa area. This organization also teaches about composting, staying safe around household pollutants, and other ways to "go green."

# READ ABOUT

These spear points were made by Native Americans in Oklahoma more than 1,000 years ago.

**9000–8000** BCE

*Early people hunt mammoths and bison in what is now Oklahoma*

▲ **5500** BCE

*Calf Creek people follow bison herds and use earthen ovens*

**1500–500** BCE

*People set up and live in seasonal camps*

# CHAPTER TWO

# FIRST PEOPLE

★

**B**ASED ON FLAKES FROM STONE TOOLS DISCOVERED IN THE REGION, ARCHAEOLOGISTS SUSPECT THAT PEOPLE FIRST CAME TO OKLAHOMA MORE THAN 12,000 YEARS AGO. Between 10,000 and 11,000 years ago, a different group of people arrived. They left behind sharp spear points that probably were used for hunting huge animals.

**500 BCE**
*Native Americans use grinding stones and the bow and arrow*

**300–800 CE**
*People in what is now Oklahoma begin planting crops*

▲**900–1400**
*Mound builders live in what is now Spiro*

Mammoth bones were found near Cooperton, not far from the Wichita Mountains. They date back more than 17,000 years!

Caddo pottery

## ANCIENT LIVES

Other big-game hunters followed. They not only pursued the mighty bison across the plain, but also herded and chased them over mountain ledges to kill them for food. Between 8,000 and 10,000 years ago, the people developed a tool that worked as both a spear and a knife. They used it to hunt deer and other smaller game.

For the next 500 years, these people continued to live off what they could hunt. And by about 5500 BCE, they merged into the Calf Creek people, as archaeologists have come to call them. The Calf Creek people followed the migrating bison herds. They developed earthen stoves for both cooking and making spearheads. Between 1500 and 500 BCE, people began setting up seasonal camps to live in. They used stones to grind tree limbs, and slowly bows and arrows began replacing spears as hunting tools. Bows and arrows allowed hunters to hunt animals from farther distances than spears could.

## CREATING SETTLEMENTS

Around 300 to 800 CE, people settled down. Rather than constantly following the herds, they took time to establish camps. As they settled, they began making pottery. Only after they had hunted all of the game and wild food in the area did the people move on.

During that same time, some people learned to plant crops of corn, beans, and squash. Because they had some control over their food supply, these groups were able to set up permanent homes. They built villages near streams and other waterways where they could fish. Within a century or two, these people had become farmers. When they had extra crops, they traded with neighboring groups.

Leaders lived in the center of the village. Villagers buried their dead in large mounds that looked like flat-topped pyramids. Archaeologists excavating these mounds have found human remains, along with quartz, jade, carved wooden masks, baskets, copper, shells, and **obsidian** blades.

## EARLY NATIVE AMERICANS

Different groups had different ways of life. Over hundreds of years, some preferred to follow their food, while others preferred staying in one spot and planting crops. Some groups traded goods with each other. They had different languages, clothing, customs, and housing. A **nomadic** family would need a house that they could easily move, whereas a farming family would need a house that could withstand different kinds of weather in one place.

### The Wichitas

Bands of Native Americans known as the Wichitas lived in the deep river valleys. They called themselves Kitikitish, which means, "tattooed eyelids." As part of their tradition, the Wichita men tattooed lines on their eyelids, and the women tattooed lines on their chins. They raised corn, which they dried and ground into meal and boiled in pots to make porridge. Their homes were dome-shaped and made out of grass thatch carefully woven around a framework of poles.

### The Caddos

The Caddos occupied the lands around the Red River in present-day Louisiana, Texas, Arkansas, and Oklahoma starting in at least 800 CE. The men and boys hunted, while the women and girls farmed,

**WORDS TO KNOW**

**obsidian** *jet-black volcanic glass*

**nomadic** *describing someone who moves from place to place and does not settle permanently in one location*

**SEE IT HERE!**

**SPIRO MOUNDS**

The mounds in Spiro offer a fascinating collection of artifacts from an ancient people. This archaeological site includes the remains of a village and 11 mounds. Archaeologists estimate that this area was a permanent settlement between 900 and 1400 CE. Visitors can get a glimpse into the lives of the Native people through the baskets, cloth, shells, and copper items that have been discovered. Where did the inhabitants of this site go? And what caused them to disappear? The answers are still a mystery.

harvesting corn, beans, and pumpkins. Typically, the men wore a long piece of animal hide between their legs, which they tucked over a belt, often with leather leggings. Women wore wraparound skirts and ponchos, usually made of deerskin. Both men and women wore buffalo robes in the winter. The men traditionally shaved their heads completely or left a strip of hair down the middle.

The Caddos lived in complex communities and were led by powerful chiefs. They thrived on growing corn and hunting deer. They grew in numbers and power until the 14th century, when severe drought shattered their agricultural base. At that point, Caddo groups scattered and moved into smaller settlements between the Red and Sabine rivers.

### The Plains Indians

The Plains Indians tended to camp in the grasslands. They were made up of several tribes, including the Lakotas, Cheyennes, Crows, and Pawnees. Men usually wore animal hide leggings, a loincloth, and a belt. A man who had shown exceptional bravery sometimes wore a grizzly bear claw around his neck. Women wore animal hide dresses and were in charge of making and decorating moccasins for the entire tribe. Living in tepees made of painted buffalo hides, the Plains groups moved around often.

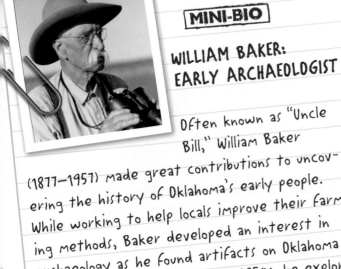

**MINI-BIO**

## WILLIAM BAKER: EARLY ARCHAEOLOGIST

Often known as "Uncle Bill," William Baker (1877–1957) made great contributions to uncovering the history of Oklahoma's early people. While working to help locals improve their farming methods, Baker developed an interest in archaeology as he found artifacts on Oklahoma farms. From the 1920s to the 1950s, he explored the Oklahoma Panhandle region and the surrounding areas. He is best known for his discoveries of arrowheads and other tools at the Nall site in southern Cimarron County. Baker was eager to learn all he could about Oklahoma's first residents, and he shared his knowledge with archaeologists throughout the United States.

**? Want to know more?** Visit www.factsfornow .scholastic.com and enter the keyword **Oklahoma**.

# Native American Settlements

## (Before European Contact)

This map shows the general area of Native American peoples before European settlers arrived.

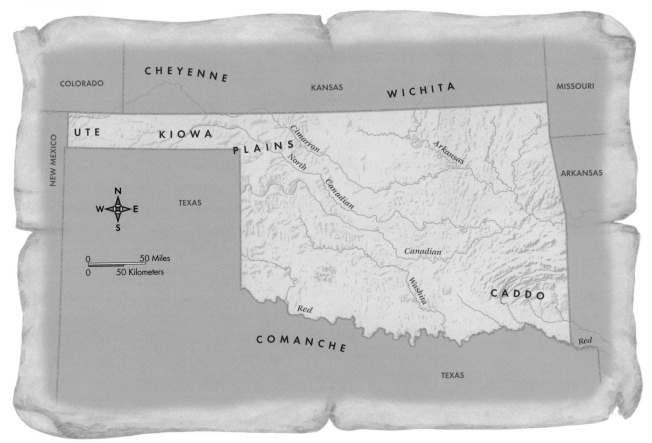

Those who stayed in one place often built dome-shaped houses of grass and dirt. The curved shape helped provide protection from severe weather.

## The Kiowas

Kiowa means "principal people." As buffalo hunters, they went wherever the herds did. Their tepees were portable, so they could move quickly and easily. Men typically wore their hair in long braids wrapped in fur

Q8 **WHERE DID THE COMANCHES GET THEIR NAME?**

A8 Some say it comes from a Ute word *Kohmahts,* which means "those who are against us." Or it could derive from the Spanish term *amino ancho,* which means "wide trail."

strips. A spot over their right ear, however, was often kept short as a symbol of their tribe. Women braided their hair or kept it long and loose. Both men and women wore moccasins, leggings, and fur robes made of animal skin.

## The Comanches

The Comanches were primarily hunter-gatherers living in southwest areas of what would become Oklahoma. They moved often and did not take time to plant crops or establish villages. They ate persimmons and other fruit, as well as various nuts and pemmican, a chewy treat made from dried meat, melted fat, and berries. The Comanches lived in tepees with four poles, designed to be taken down quickly for traveling.

## The Utes

The Utes lived in villages in the hills and depended less on hunting and more on trading with other people. They traded for roots, fruits, corn, and herbs. Their name means "land of the sun" and is the source of the state of Utah's name. The Utes' homes, called wicki-ups, were bark-covered, domelike huts. The people wore pants and dresses made out of deer skin as well

The Comanches lived in tepees such as these. The tepees could be taken down and moved as needed.

A Ute wickiup

as smaller animals like minks and jackrabbits. Their spiritual beliefs were based on nature, and they saw the bear as a powerful force. Their legends often centered on the bear, and once a year, the Ute would gather for the Momaqui Mowat, or the Beardance.

## STRANGERS ON THE HORIZON

Native Americans thrived for many centuries in the area we now call Oklahoma. However, their ways of life and their homeland were about to change drastically, as strangers from Spain and France arrived.

## Picture Yourself . . .

### Making a Spear

Today, the sky is clear, and you know it is time to hunt for the perfect piece of rock. You take your sharpened stick and go to a rock bed. You search for a long time. The stone must be perfect. The sun sparkles on a piece of flint, and you know your search is over. It is just what you need. It is brittle and breaks easily. You take a hammerstone and chip off large flakes until your flint is the pointed shape that you want it to be. Using a piece of deer antler, you remove smaller pieces until your flint is pointed and very sharp. Later, after your father has seen your work, you will attach it to the spear handle that you readied weeks ago. You go to bed dreaming of the game animals you will hunt.

## READ ABOUT

Francisco Vásquez de Coronado and his expedition traveling through the Southwest

**1541**

Francisco Vásquez de Coronado reaches the region and claims it for Spain

▲**1682**

La Salle claims the Louisiana region for France

**1718**

Jean-Baptiste Bérnard de La Harpe establish trading posts along th Red River

CHAPTER THREE

# EXPLORATION AND SETTLEMENT

★

I N 1541, THE FIRST EUROPEANS SET FOOT IN WHAT IS NOW OKLAHOMA. Spanish explorer Francisco Vásquez de Coronado traveled through a part of Oklahoma in search of treasures in the Great Plains. When Coronado carved his name and the date on a rock near the Cimarron River, it marked the beginning of Oklahoma's recorded history.

**1759**

*The Wichitas and their Comanche allies defeat Colonel Diego Ortiz Parrilla's forces*

▲**1762**

*France cedes its Louisiana territory, including Oklahoma, to Spain*

**1775–1783**

*The Revolutionary War is fought*

René-Robert Cavelier, Sieur de La Salle

## INTRODUCTION OF THE HORSE

When Francisco Vásquez de Coronado departed from the region, he left some horses behind. These animals quickly became an important part of Indian life. Indians used them to track buffalo across the Great Plains, as well as for hunting and fighting. The Comanches, known as the Lords of the Plains, became excellent horsemen, teaching even small children to ride. They based their wealth on how many horses they owned. Coronado and his expedition didn't establish any settlements there, but their horses changed Oklahoma forever.

## SPANISH EXPLORERS

Coronado and his huge group of men, armored horses, and pack mules must have appeared intimidating to the Native Americans. These Spanish explorers had found great riches in Mexico and had heard a story that there was a golden city to the north. When they reached the current city of Quivira, they expected to find women serving beverages from golden pitchers and golden bells hanging from trees. But instead, they found people with tattoos who lived in grass huts.

Another Spanish explorer who may have reached present-day Oklahoma was Hernando de Soto. He traveled through North America from 1539 to 1542. He and others may not have found treasure, but they kept diaries and other written records of their activities. By studying these documents, historians have learned a great deal about the people in this region at that time.

During their travels, the Spanish unintentionally introduced diseases that killed many Native Americans. European illnesses swept through the area unchecked, infecting many who had no immunity against them. These diseases devastated Oklahoma's Native American population.

## ARRIVAL OF THE FRENCH

In 1679, French explorers led by René-Robert Cavelier, Sieur de La Salle, set out in canoes from the Great Lakes. When La Salle and his party reached the mouth of the Mississippi in 1682, he claimed the entire region—from the Mississippi River to the Rocky Mountains and the Gulf of Mexico to Canada—for France. He named it Louisiana after King Louis XIV.

Unlike the Spanish, the French wanted to make use of the land they were exploring. The Indians of east-

# European Exploration of Oklahoma

The colored arrows on this map show the routes taken by European explorers between 1539 and 1719.

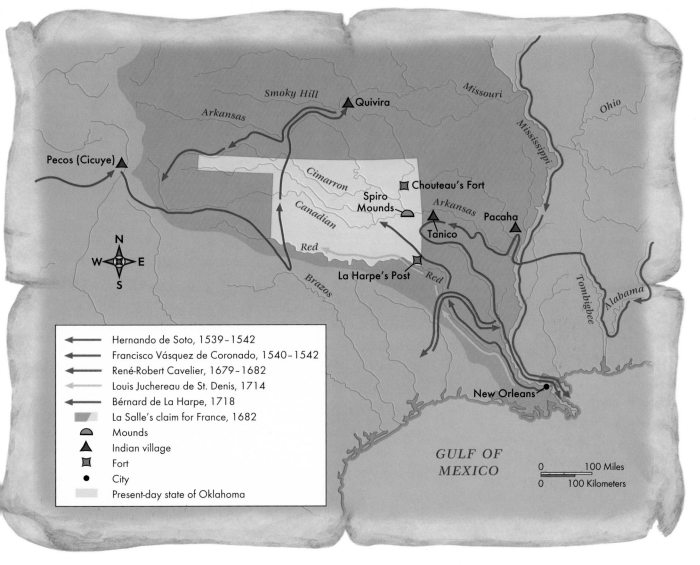

Smoky Hill

Missouri

Arkansas

Ohio

Mississippi

Quivira

Pecos (Cicuye)

Cimarron

Chouteau's Fort

Spiro Mounds

Arkansas

Canadian

Tanico

Pacaha

Red

La Harpe's Post

Red

Brazos

Tombigbee

Alabama

New Orleans

**Legend:**
- Hernando de Soto, 1539–1542
- Francisco Vásquez de Coronado, 1540–1542
- René-Robert Cavelier, 1679–1682
- Louis Juchereau de St. Denis, 1714
- Bérnard de La Harpe, 1718
- La Salle's claim for France, 1682
- Mounds
- Indian village
- Fort
- City
- Present-day state of Oklahoma

**GULF OF MEXICO**

0    100 Miles
0    100 Kilometers

ern North America had been providing French traders with beaver, otter, mink, and muskrat **pelts**. These furs were fashionable in Europe and were very valuable. In return, the French provided the Native Americans with silver, knives, mirrors, sugar, guns, and ammunition.

**WORD TO KNOW**

**pelts** *animal skins covered in fur*

Louis Juchereau de St. Denis arrived in 1714 and began trading with the Native Americans.

## Picture Yourself . . .

### as a French Explorer in the 1700s

You are tired from a long journey from the north. You have paddled your canoe for weeks, searching for new trading partners. You suddenly come across a group of people whose clothes, customs, and ways of life are unfamiliar to you. You offer them gifts. Your guide kills a deer, and you share the meat with the Native Americans you have just met. You try to earn their trust so they will trade their furs, skins, and other items with you. If you are successful, you may decide to stay and build a home in the region.

The first Frenchman to set foot in what is now Oklahoma was Louis Juchereau de St. Denis. In 1714, he sailed up into Oklahoma on the Red River and established trading posts along the river's banks with the Native Americans. In 1718, another Frenchman named Jean-Baptiste Bérnard de La Harpe also established trading posts along the Red River, and he described his encounters with Oklahoma's Native Americans in his journal. In particular, La Harpe made contact with Caddo and Wichita farmers. They planted corn, pumpkin, and other crops in the spring and hunted buffalo on horseback in the fall. Just as La Salle had done years before, La Harpe claimed the area for France.

By the mid-1700s, Wichita villages along the Red River served as trading posts for French traders. The French built and established towns, traded with the Native Americans, and married Indian women. The French used the Red, Arkansas, Canadian, and Grand rivers to transport their newly acquired furs, buffalo skins, and other goods to the markets in Europe. It was a time of great prosperity for both the French and the Native Americans.

## CHANGES IN THE REGION

Although the Wichitas got along with the French traders, they didn't care for Spanish missionaries who had established missions to the south, in Texas and northern Mexico. The Wichitas occasionally attacked those settlements. In an attempt to put an end to this trouble, in 1759 Spanish colonel Diego Ortiz Parrilla made his way north to the Red River with 360 soldiers and volunteers and 176 Apaches. The Wichita warriors, together with their Comanche allies, attacked the Spanish army. In its flight, the Spanish army had to leave behind two cannons, which turned out to be useless in the deep sand on the banks of the Red River.

## A NEW NATION

In 1762, France ceded its Louisiana Territory, including Oklahoma, to Spain. So Oklahoma was officially Spanish during the Revolutionary War (1775–1783), in which the American colonies gained independence from Great Britain and the United States was born. As the nation gained strength, more and more people decided to explore the lands to the west. These new settlers created conflict with the Native Americans who had been on the land for thousands of years.

Spaniards celebrate gaining the Louisiana Territory.

## AN EXPLORER'S JOURNAL

Jean-Baptiste Bérnard de La Harpe (1683–1765) spent a great deal of time exploring the Arkansas River valley and what is now the eastern part of Oklahoma. He recorded his observations about the Native Americans he encountered and the natural landmarks he saw. One journal entry reads, "We came into a beautiful prairie, varied by hills and thickets; we found there a prodigious quantity of wild cattle, and a great number of wolves; they are little and not at all bad. We saw there, also, some partridges, of woodcock and of plover. The evening we mounted to the summit of a rock, on descending from which we camped near a little lake." His journal has helped historians learn about Native Americans and the land as well as European ideas from this time.

## READ ABOUT

This map shows
the Louisiana
Territory and the
area that became
the state of
Oklahoma.

British
Possessions

Louisiana
Purchase

Spanish
Possessions

N
W E
S

| | United States, 1803 |
| | Louisiana Purchase |
| | United States Territory, 1803 |
| | Present-day state of Oklahoma |

**1803** ▶

*President Thomas
Jefferson purchases the
Louisiana Territory for
the United States*

**1830**

*President Andrew Jackson
signs the Indian Removal Act,
creating Indian Territory*

**1862**

*Congress passes the
Homestead Act*

CHAPTER FOUR

# GROWTH AND CHANGE

★

S PAIN RETURNED THE LOUISIANA TERRITORY TO FRANCE IN 1800. The American Revolution was over, the U.S. Constitution was in place, and the United States was on the brink of tremendous growth. In 1803, President Thomas Jefferson made the best real estate deal in history when he bought the huge Louisiana Territory from France.

▲ **1865–1886**
*Cattle drives move through Indian Territory*

**1896**
*The first commercial oil well in Oklahoma is drilled*

**1907** ▶
*Oklahoma becomes the 46th state*

## TRAIL OF TEARS

More and more people were arriving in the United States from all over the world. Land was in high demand. It soon became clear to the U.S. government that in order to provide land for all of the incoming settlers, it would have to force the eastern Native Americans to move west.

In 1830, President Andrew Jackson signed the Indian Removal Act. He and then president Martin Van Buren ordered the U.S. Army to drive the Indian nations of the eastern seaboard to an "Indian Territory" in Oklahoma. One U.S. Army private wrote, "I saw the helpless Cherokees arrested and dragged from their

The Trail of Tears, as painted by artist Robert Ottokar Lindneux

# SEMINOLES JOHN HORSE AND WILD CAT: FREEDOM FIGHTERS

A courageous battle for freedom was waged for years by the Seminole Nation, a mixture of Native Americans and African Americans. The Seminoles fought invasions of Florida for 42 years. During the Trail of Tears, Seminole families were sent to live in Oklahoma's Indian Territory. By then, they were led by Wild Cat (Coacoochee), a Native Seminole, and John Horse, a black Seminole. Both men were 25 when they met. They became good friends and agreed to keep their multicultural nation unified.

In the Oklahoma Indian Territory, Horse and Wild Cat founded the town of Wewoka. Their armed forces protected Seminole families from raids by slave catchers. But in 1849, the raids increased, and the two men led their people in an **exodus** through Texas. In late 1850, they led the Seminoles across the Rio Grande into Mexico.

homes, and driven by bayonet [to Oklahoma]. And in the chill of a drizzling rain on an October morning I saw them loaded like cattle or sheep into wagons and started toward the west." Along with the Indians on this Trail of Tears were thousands of African Americans, some enslaved and others free.

Few Indian nations moved willingly. Some, like the Seminoles and the Cherokees, fought exile but were forced out. They made the trip of more than 2,000 miles (3,200 km) on foot. A Seminole leader described the removal of his people from Florida to Oklahoma: "[We were] transported to a cold climate, naked, without game to hunt, or fields to plant, or huts to cover our poor children; they are crying like wolves, hungry, cold, and destitute." Tens of thousands began the voyage in 1838, but far fewer survived. Many died from starvation, frostbite, and disease. One-third of all Cherokees died.

These were Native American nations with advanced systems of education, law enforcement, and government. Despite the devastation, as each nation reached Oklahoma, it immediately began to set up towns, places of worship, schools, and businesses. The Plains nations were elbowed aside as the Native American **diaspora** landed penniless in this unknown land.

## WORDS TO KNOW

**exodus** *a mass departure from an area*

**diaspora** *the movement and scattering of people away from their homeland*

African American soldiers played a vital role in the Battle of Honey Springs in July 1863.

## GOVERNMENT TACTICS

To remove Native Americans from their lands, the U.S. government used tactics such as bribery, false promises, broken treaties, and outright threats. They bribed the Native Americans with thousands of dollars worth of food and liquor. When the bribes didn't work, the government promised the Indians millions of acres in what are now Arkansas and Oklahoma, as well as guns, ammunition, food, and other items. Finally, the legislature enacted laws that took away all Indian rights and made U.S. claims to the land legal. And when Native Americans refused to leave, they were forcibly removed from their land.

## THE CIVIL WAR

In 1860, Abraham Lincoln was elected president. Fearful that he would end slavery, 11 Southern states left the Union. This action led to the Civil War, a conflict between the North (the Union) and the South (the Confederacy). The leaders of the Five Nations (Cherokee, Creek, Chickasaw, Choctaw, and Seminole) were surrounded on three sides by Confederate armed forces. Under pressure from these forces, the Five Nations agreed to support the Confederacy.

But in August 1861, wealthy Creek chief Opothle Yahola offered freedom to all who joined him in a march to Kansas. Some 5,000 Creeks, 2,500 Seminoles, 500 Cherokees, and 500 slaves from these nations took up his offer. In the dead of winter, and pursued by the Confederate cavalry, Yahola led thousands toward Union lines in Kansas. Three times, his people fought off military attacks. They finally staggered on to Kansas. By April 1862, about 200 of his young men had joined the Union army, becoming the first soldiers of color to fight the Confederacy. They raided Missouri plantations to liberate their sisters and brothers.

Fighting alongside the Native Americans were African Americans. They became an important factor in the Union's victory. The Battle of Honey Springs took place on July 17, 1863, in Indian Territory in what is today eastern Oklahoma. The African American presence there was the key to the Union's victory. On a small battlefield just outside present-day Muskogee, African American troops held their line, and the Union won. At this decisive battle, the Union gained control of the Arkansas River and the Texas Road. These were key transportation routes.

## THE RACE FOR LAND

In 1862, Congress passed the Homestead Act, which granted families 160 acres (65 ha) of land in the central and western states if they promised to live on the land for five years. People arrived in Oklahoma in growing numbers. A few years later, much of Indian Territory was called Unassigned Lands. To encourage white families to move west, promoters called "boomers" were sought to persuade families, farmers, and businesses to pack up and go. Some boomers were so convincing that thousands of people left for Oklahoma.

A family of homesteaders traveling by wagon to claim newly available land

## BIRTH OF THE AMERICAN COWBOY

After the Civil War, a new kind of Oklahoma invasion began: cattle. There was a growing demand for beef nationwide. Ranchers hired cowboys to herd cattle from Texas to the north. Long, winding cattle trails named the Chisholm, Western, and Old Shawnee saw the passage of millions of cattle from the Red River through north-central Oklahoma to Kansas. Often the pathways were so crowded with the pounding hooves of cattle and horses that new trails had to be created just to find enough room for all of them. Throughout the spring and summer, trail-driving outfits rode with thousands of cattle. These groups would include a boss and 10 to 15 helpers, a cook, plus at least half a dozen horses and several wagons. Typically, a team would travel about 10 to 12 miles (16 to 19 km) a day, stopping only for a traditional meal of bread, meat, beans with bacon, and coffee. Between 1865 and 1886, cowboys drove more than 6 million longhorn cattle from Texas across Oklahoma to the railroads in Kansas. They developed skills that would eventually amaze rodeo crowds.

## MINI-BIO

### BILL PICKETT: THE DUSKY DEMON

Bill Pickett (1870–1932) entertained people for years with the rodeo sport he invented—"bulldogging," or steer wrestling. For 40 years, this talented African American starred in Oklahoma's 101 Ranch Rodeos. When a huge steer was released, Pickett would grab it by the horns and wrestle it to the ground. He was known as "The Dusky Demon," and in 1922 he made a movie featuring his famous act.

**? Want to know more?** Visit www.factsfornow.scholastic.com and enter the keyword **Oklahoma**.

Judge Isaac Parker

## EXPANDING SETTLEMENTS

By the 1870s, railroads crossed through Oklahoma, making the land accessible to more people. The railroad made it possible to travel across the state in just a few hours. All kinds of people were now attracted to Oklahoma—brave sheriffs and evil outlaws, schoolteachers and homesteaders. The expanding settlements turned land once home to many Native Americans into ranches, shops, and stores.

Such tremendous growth and change brought its share of crime and conflict. Like many other frontier states, Oklahoma's approach to law and order was homemade. It boasted some of the worst outlaws in history, and some of the best lawmen. Judge Isaac Parker arrived in 1875 and appointed 200 Native Americans, African Americans, and whites as deputy marshals. They faced a host of cattle rustlers, vicious outlaws, and young men who slipped into a life of crime. There were bands of criminals such as the Dick Glass gang, the Bill Cook gang, and the Rufus Buck gang. And there was Cherokee Bill, a black Cherokee who fired off so many shots that it rattled anyone who went after him. Judge Parker finally caught up with this one-man crime wave.

## LAND RUNS

In 1889, the U.S. government divided the Indian Territory into two parts. The eastern section was for Indians. The western portion became the Oklahoma Territory. Although Native Americans were given a lot of land on reservations, the U.S. government kept buying it. One Kiowa leader named Lone Wolf protested all the way to the Supreme Court. But the judges declared that the government had the right to break Indian treaties.

Perhaps more than any other state in the Union, Oklahoma was born in a disorderly but highly American way: with six huge "land runs" that settled massive areas, each in a single day. People came from all over on horses, on mules, in wagons, and even on foot to take part in the first Oklahoma land rush on April 22, 1889. When the U.S. Army fired its cannon to start the rush, an estimated 100,000 people stampeded for what was once Indian land. This rush included 10,000 African Americans. By April 23, 10,000 non-Indian people turned Oklahoma City into a city of tents, and 15,000 others had done the same in Guthrie.

Settlers raced for territory during the Oklahoma land rush of 1889.

## WOW

One of Judge Isaac Parker's best lawmen was Bass Reaves, an African American who devoted 37 years of his life to tracking down Oklahoma's worst outlaws. Only one man, Hullabee Smith, ever escaped from Reaves.

Some people were so eager for the land run that they could not wait. Many snuck through early. These people were nicknamed "Sooners" because they came in too soon. Today, Oklahoma is called the Sooner State.

From 1867 to 1898, African American soldiers stationed at Fort Sill and Fort Gibson built forts in the newly settled territory, kept an eye on borders, and fought off thieves. They brought law and order to the Indian Territory. Some of them had Indian ancestors, but they were not heroes to the Native Americans because they carried out U.S. government rulings regarding the Indians. In some instances, they were able to protect Indians from **desperadoes**. Native Americans named these men buffalo soldiers because their dark, curly hair resembled that of the buffalo.

Advertisements handed out throughout the South encouraged African Americans to come to Oklahoma and create cities and businesses—or even the first black state. Edwin P. McCabe persuaded tens of thousands of

## WORD TO KNOW

**desperadoes** *bold or violent criminals, usually in the 19th-century western United States*

Buffalo soldiers as seen in a Frederic Remington engraving

African American families to settle in Oklahoma. In his newspaper, the *Langston Herald*, he asked, "What will you be if you stay in the South? Slaves liable to be killed at any time, and never treated right: but if you come to Oklahoma you have equal chances with the white man, free and independent." Between 1890 and 1910, African Americans founded 32 black towns. These towns had black sheriffs, teachers, doctors, and store and hotel owners. The pride of each black town was its educational system. These schools raised the literacy rate of formerly enslaved children to more than 90 percent.

## EDWIN P. MCCABE: FOUNDER OF LANGSTON CITY

Edwin P. McCabe (1850-1920), an African American with Indian ancestry, wanted to help the mistreated people of the Southern states. Beginning with the Oklahoma land run in 1889, he devised a rescue plan. He purchased the land to found Langston City. His dream was to bring Southern black families to Oklahoma where they would find freedom and justice. If enough families arrived, they might be able to elect representatives who would make it a black U.S. state. He established the Langston Herald to promote immigration and civic pride.

But in 1907, Oklahoma entered the Union as another **segregated** Southern state. McCabe left to live out his life in Chicago.

**? Want to know more?** Visit www.factsfornow.scholastic.com and enter the keyword **Oklahoma**.

## WORD TO KNOW

**segregated** *set apart or separated from others by group or race*

The residents of Grant, an African American town, in 1904

**The opening of the Cherokee Strip in Oklahoma Territory, 1893**

The last great land opening in the American West took place in 1901 by lottery, or random drawing. The lottery opened the Kiowa, Comanche, Apache, and Wichita reservations to non-Indian settlement. More than 165,000 settlers entered their names for 13,000 homesteads of 160 acres (65 ha) each.

# Oklahoma: From Territory to Statehood

This map shows the original Oklahoma Territory and the area (in orange) that became the state of Oklahoma in 1907.

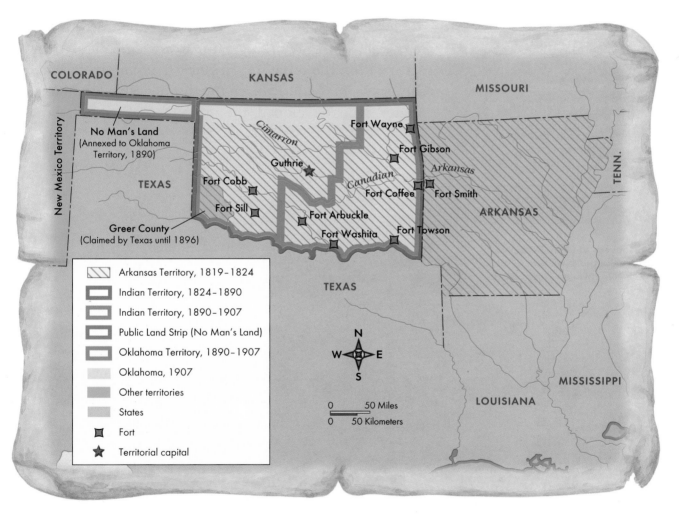

## BECOMING A STATE

In 1900, the population of Oklahoma stood at 800,000. Seven years later, it was 1.4 million owing to the rush from the east for land and oil. The first commercial oil well in Oklahoma was drilled in 1896 in Bartlesville.

## THE TOWN OF BOLEY

The African American town of Boley, Oklahoma, was founded in 1904 in Indian Territory. It was established on 160 acres (65 ha) of land owned by Abigail Barnett McCormick, a black Choctaw. At one time, 4,000 people lived in Boley, making it the most populated black town in the country. Half of its high school graduates went on to college, and Creek Seminole College was built on 80 acres (32 ha) there.

Fewer than one out of five Oklahomans were Native Americans. In the Oklahoma Territory, there were 19,000 African Americans, and about double that number lived in the Indian Territory. Of the 32 black towns in Oklahoma, all but five were in Indian Territory.

As Oklahoma moved toward statehood, its Native Americans were working hard to develop their own state within the territory. In 1905, five nations formed the state of Sequoyah, named after the Cherokee leader who developed the first Cherokee alphabet.

The discovery of oil in Oklahoma helped make the state prosperous. Oil wells like this one were built in many areas.

They adopted a constitution and brought it to the U.S. Congress, but the federal government refused to acknowledge it.

On November 16, 1907, President Theodore Roosevelt officially made Oklahoma the 46th state.

President Theodore Roosevelt signed Oklahoma into statehood on November 16, 1907. It was the 46th state admitted to the Union. Its population far exceeded the minimum of 60,000 that was required for statehood. The state capital was originally set in Guthrie, but three years later it was moved to Oklahoma City.

# READ ABOUT

A gushing
oil well near
Oklahoma City

**1921**

A race riot erupts in the
city of Tulsa

▲ **1930s**

The Dust Bowl
devastates the plains

**1970**

The McClellan-Kerr
Arkansas River
Navigation System is
completed

# CHAPTER FIVE

# MORE MODERN TIMES

★

AS THE 20TH CENTURY BEGAN, OIL WAS BECOMING A PRECIOUS RESOURCE. By 1905, you could find cowhands working on vast ranches on the outskirts of Tulsa, "the Oil Capital of the World." By the time Oklahoma became a state, so many oil deposits had been discovered that Oklahoma was set to become the largest oil-producing state in the country.

**▲1995**
The Murrah Federal Building in Oklahoma City is bombed

**1999**
*Dozens of tornadoes sweep the state, causing billions of dollars in damage*

**2013**
*A tornado strikes the town of Moore, killing 24 people and injuring hundreds of others*

## FRANK PHILLIPS: FROM BANKER TO OILMAN

Frank Phillips (1873–1950) was born on a farm in Nebraska and raised in Iowa. As a young man, he moved to New England to work as a banker. His ambition eventually drove him back to Bartlesville, Oklahoma. Phillips and his brother Lee Eldas (known as L. E.) began a bank and invested in oil wells around the area. They began drilling wells on Osage land, with the Indians' permission. After a few failed attempts, Phillips finally struck oil—on 81 different wells! The Osages, thankful for the revenue he brought into the region, made Phillips an honorary leader. He went on to found the Phillips Petroleum Co. in 1917, and opened up gas stations all over the country.

**? Want to know more?** Visit www.factsfornow .scholastic.com and enter the keyword **Oklahoma**.

## EARLY OIL

In the early 1820s, when Native Americans skimmed the black, sticky element from the surface of some water sources with a feather, they were gathering medicine. They thought it would help to heal painful disorders of the joints and muscles. It turns out they were dealing with "black gold," oil that would one day become the state's greatest source of income.

## BLACK GOLD

From farmers to land prospectors, everyone was drilling wells into the ground hoping to strike it rich by hitting oil, or "black gold." Sure enough, as more wells were drilled, more oil was found, turning people into millionaires overnight. The sudden, fabulous wealth also turned some people into criminals. A corrupt Tulsa government allowed illegal gambling and drinking and did practically nothing to combat robberies of shops and banks.

## TROUBLE IN TULSA

The country was growing and expanding toward new horizons—some better, some worse. In 1917, U.S. troops began fighting in World War I. In order to feed them, the government bought wheat from Oklahoma farmers. This helped the state's economy grow stronger, providing jobs for farmers and tax revenues for the state.

**One oil deposit discovered in Oklahoma City in 1928 began gushing oil straight up in the air at dizzying rates. Almost 20,000 barrels a day were splashing all over the ground until the well was finally capped!**

By the time World War I ended in 1918, it had been the most violent war in human history. White American soldiers returned home in search of jobs, and many did not like competing with African Americans for work. Riots struck a number of cities across the country, with the worst rocking Tulsa in 1921.

Tulsa was different from other cities in that oil had made many blacks wealthy, which stung some of the city's poor whites. In addition, most Oklahomans were pioneers from other states. Some of them believed that whites were superior to other races. They fiercely disagreed with black Oklahomans' demands for equality. Most black Oklahomans had worked hard to leave southern states and ways behind. They had little or no tolerance for racists.

**Many oil wells gushed oil along with natural gas, which is flammable. No one was allowed to start a fire or light a match within miles of a well.**

**A view of Tulsa after World War I**

After the 1921 riots, many neighborhoods were left destroyed.

Taken together, these attitudes turned a misstep into a citywide disaster. On May 30, 1921, a black man accidentally stepped on a white woman's foot. When the woman claimed that he had attacked her, authorities put him in jail. Given Tulsa's weak justice department, its black community feared for the young man's life. Rumors quickly spread, and later that night whites and blacks exchanged gunfire outside the jail.

By dawn the next morning, a mob of more than 10,000 whites attacked the black neighborhood known as Little Africa. Many people died, some in burning buildings, some by machine-gun fire. It took the Oklahoma National Guard to control the riot. According to a magazine article from the summer of 1921, "on Wednesday and Thursday the Salvation Army fed thirty-seven [blacks] employed as grave diggers and twenty on Friday and Saturday. During the first two days these men dug 120 graves in each of which a dead [black person] was buried." To this day, it is not known how many people lost their lives in the Tulsa riot, one of the lowest points in Oklahoma's history.

## GET YOUR KICKS!

Route 66 is a 2,400-mile (3,900 km) highway reaching across much of the country. It began, however, in Oklahoma. The road is so famous that a song was written about it. Some of the lyrics say, "Get your kicks on Route 66."

A Tulsa businessman named Cyrus Avery helped create the U.S. highway system in 1926. He pushed for a road that would go all the way from Chicago, Illinois, to Los Angeles, California, dipping south through Oklahoma before turning west. For decades, Route 66 was the highway to travel. But that changed when the interstate freeways entered the picture. In 1989, the Oklahoma legislature agreed that this historic highway had to be preserved. Historic markers were put up and efforts were made to lure travelers to the "Main Street of America." Today, Route 66 is still popular. Of its original total miles, approximately 80 percent are still drivable. Although speeds are slower than on some highways, Route 66 is rich with sightseeing opportunities. Almost 400 miles (650 km) of the legendary highway pass through Oklahoma.

## REMEMBERING THE RIOTS

Pioneering historian John Hope Franklin recalled how the notorious 1921 race riot affected his family. His father had just taken up residence in Tulsa. After the riot, young John, his mother, and his siblings were prevented from joining him there. The devastation of Tulsa's black community at the hands of white mobs delayed the family's reunion for a number of years. John's father worked in Tulsa to establish a viable law practice. Franklin's mother worked as a teacher and raised her children in Rentiesville, Oklahoma, until it became possible to reunite the family.

In an April 2007 interview, Franklin explained, "There are people, even when I go back to Tulsa, who claim they hadn't heard of the riots until they were grown. And maybe that's so, but the conspiracy of silence has been what has kept the history of this country distorted and misrepresented."

## A TRYING DECADE

Oil production would not be enough to provide for Oklahomans during the Great Depression. In 1929, the New York Stock Exchange crashed. Businesses and banks closed. People lost their savings and their jobs. Work was scarce, and food was hard to come by. As if that wasn't bad enough, things were going to get worse for Oklahoma and the Great Plains.

In 1933, a severe drought hit the Great Plains. In previous years, farmers had plowed up the deep-rooted prairie grasses to plant wheat and corn. Without the prairie grasses, there was nothing to hold the dirt in place once the rain stopped and the wind arrived. Immense dust clouds engulfed parts of Oklahoma. Some dust clouds were more than 5 miles high (8 km) and blocked out the sun. An eyewitness described such a cloud:

A huge dust cloud engulfs a farm in Boise City, in 1935.

These Oklahomans lost their farm when a drought destroyed the crops.

"It has the banked appearance of a cumulus cloud, but it is black instead of white, and it hangs low, seeming to hug the earth. Instead of being slow to change its form, it appears to be rolling on itself from the crest downward. As it sweeps onward, the landscape is progressively blotted out."

## WOODY GUTHRIE: SONGWRITER

Woody Guthrie (1912–1967) is one of America's most beloved folksingers. Born in Okemah, Guthrie traveled a lot as he looked for work during the Dust Bowl and the Great Depression. On his travels, he saw what Americans were facing each day. And he was particularly interested in the needs of the working class. So when he turned to music, his songs often spoke of poverty and everyday people. Eventually, he wrote more than 1,000 songs, including many for children. He once said, "I am out to sing songs that will prove to you that this is your world and that if it has hit you pretty hard and knocked you for a dozen loops, no matter what color, what size you are, how you are built, I am out to sing the songs that make you take pride in yourself and in your work."

**? Want to know more?** Visit www.factsfornow .scholastic.com and enter the keyword **Oklahoma**.

## REMEMBERING THE STORM

"Birds fly in terror before the storm, and only those that are strong of wing may escape. The smaller birds fly until they are exhausted, then fall to the ground, to share the fate of the thousands of jack rabbits which perish from suffocation."
—Dust storm described by eyewitness Lawrence Svobida, 1930s

In the 1930s, the Works Progress Administration sponsored this road construction project between Tulsa and Sand Springs.

## FAQ

**Q8 WHAT HAPPENED TO THE CIVILIAN CONSERVATION CORPS?**

**A8** The CCC existed for nine years, until June 1942, when it was absorbed into the armed forces.

Both the Great Depression and the Dust Bowl contributed to the extremely difficult decade of the 1930s in Oklahoma. Almost 40,000 people left the state.

Public works projects were started as a direct result of President Franklin D. Roosevelt's New Deal. The New Deal was a series of programs he instituted between 1933 and 1938. The goal of the New Deal was relief, recovery, and reform of the U.S. economy during the Great Depression. Some of the programs in Oklahoma were the Works Progress Administration (WPA) and the Civilian Conservation Corps (CCC). The WPA built schools and other public buildings, sponsored artists who painted historic murals, and even financed the Oklahoma State Symphony. The CCC employed more than 100,000 Oklahomans and helped establish six state parks and about 100 campgrounds. They also built hiking trails, roads, and dams throughout the state.

## WORLD WAR II

Things changed when World War II began in Europe in 1939. The economy began to look up as the state produced coal and oil for America's allies, as well as food and other supplies for their troops. The Japanese attack on Pearl Harbor brought the United States into the war in 1941. Oklahoma's population grew with the many military personnel who came to Fort Sill, near Lawton, for training. Oklahomans went to work building airfields and military bases. Oilman Robert S. Kerr became Oklahoma's governor in 1942. During the war, he led the state in expanding business and getting out of debt.

## INDUSTRY AND CHANGE

After World War II ended in 1945, Oklahoma focused on building its plastics, electronics, and space equipment industries. Dams were built to prevent flooding and to provide power to homes and businesses. In 1947, the legislature authorized construction of the Turner Turnpike, which connected Oklahoma's two largest cities, Oklahoma City and Tulsa, when it was completed in 1953. The construction of a highway system improved interstate transportation and helped bring newcomers to the area.

Oil production increased, peaking in the mid-1950s. Eventually, the state would have more than 84,000 oil wells, as well as 32,000 natural gas wells.

During the 1950s and 1960s, the civil rights movement was bringing about change throughout the country. This was true in Oklahoma as well. Most lunch counters and restaurants in the state had been segregated, with black and white people having to eat in separate areas. In Oklahoma

**The Tulsa entrance to the Turner Turnpike**

ONC-66—Tulsa Entrance to the Turner Turnpike, Tulsa, Oklahoma

TURNER TURNPIKE

City, some people decided to protest. Inspired by Martin Luther King Jr. and other civil rights leaders, they staged **sit-ins** and eventually brought an end to this practice.

In 1970, the McClellan-Kerr Arkansas River Navigation System was completed. It gave the state the structure for a rising shipping industry and provided a source of hydroelectric power and jobs. After the 1970s, when oil production dipped again, the state focused on developing manufacturing and other industries. Oklahoma continued its economic growth through the 1990s, but a horrific disaster hit in 1995.

## OKLAHOMA CITY BOMBING

On April 19, 1995, the entire world looked at Oklahoma in horror and grief. In an act of terrorism, a man named Timothy McVeigh parked a 20-foot (6 m) truck outside the Alfred P. Murrah Federal Building in Oklahoma City. It was loaded with 5,000 pounds (2,300 kg) of explosives. At 9:02 AM, it blew up. The explosion killed 168 people and injured about 800. It was one of Oklahoma's, and America's, worst terror attacks.

These visitors to the Oklahoma City National Memorial walk among empty chairs that symbolize the victims of the Oklahoma City bombing.

In 2001, a memorial was erected to remember the innocent people who died. At the 10-year anniversary of the bombing, Vice President Dick Cheney said, "The United States has known times of sadness both before and after the Murrah building was attacked. Yet, that spring morning 10 years ago is still deeply etched in our memories. We want to remember April 19, 1995, not merely because great evil appeared that day, but because goodness overcame evil that day." President Bill Clinton, who was in office at the time of the bombing, added, "Ten years later, we still grieve and remember. But we should be very proud that Oklahoma was not paralyzed by its pain."

## OKLAHOMA TODAY

Much has changed in Oklahoma since the tough days of the Dust Bowl. The state still faces challenges, including severe weather. In 1999, an outbreak of 74 tornadoes swept through the state in a single day, damaging thousands of homes and injuring hundreds of people. In May 2013, one of the most powerful tornadoes in state history hammered the town of Moore and its surrounding area. Winds blew at speeds of more than 200 miles per hour as the tornado grew to a width of 1.3 miles. The disastrous storm killed 24 people and caused around $2 billion of damage to the buildings caught in its pathway. Support for the residents of Moore poured in from around the nation. Though the town was devastated by the tornado, it is beginning to recover and rebuild. Even in the face of tragedy, Oklahomans have much to be proud of. The state remains a powerful cultural force in the Great Plains region and shows many signs of continued prosperity.

# READ ABOUT

Oklahoma State
football fans cheer
on their team
during a 2012
game against the
Savannah State
Tigers.

# PEOPLE

★

OKLAHOMA RESIDENTS CAN TRACE THEIR ROOTS TO PLACES ALL OVER THE GLOBE—NEAR AND FAR. Some have ancestors who arrived long before there was a state called Oklahoma. Others have barely unpacked. Some were forced to settle there, while others went because they wanted to. Today, Oklahomans live in big cities and on small farms. They work in hospitals and schools, sports arenas and art galleries. Oklahoma is a great place to call home.

A young Cheyenne boy attends the Red Earth Festival in Oklahoma City.

## A LAND OF DIVERSITY

More Native Americans live in Oklahoma than in almost any other state in the country. Of the 3,751,351 people living in Oklahoma, about 8 percent are Native American. Most are descended from the 67 tribes that once lived in Indian Territory. Today, the state contains the tribal headquarters of 39 nations.

In cities and towns throughout the state, public murals, sculptures, and other works of art depict the history of the different Native American nations that came to Oklahoma. Many cities, streets, and neighborhoods take their names from Choctaw, Cherokee, and other Indian languages. And there are museums that display the artifacts and explore the rich cultures of Oklahoma's Native people.

# People QuickFacts

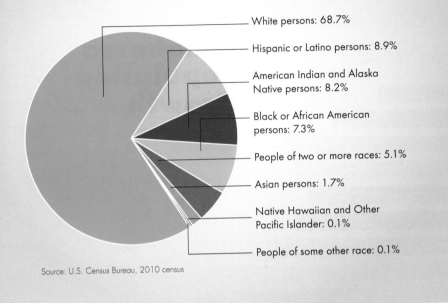

White persons: 68.7%

Hispanic or Latino persons: 8.9%

American Indian and Alaska Native persons: 8.2%

Black or African American persons: 7.3%

People of two or more races: 5.1%

Asian persons: 1.7%

Native Hawaiian and Other Pacific Islander: 0.1%

People of some other race: 0.1%

Source: U.S. Census Bureau, 2010 census

Many African American Oklahomans are descendants of enslaved people, cowboys, settlers, and farmers who first came to the area after Indians were resettled in the West. When the Depression ended, many African Americans left small towns and rural areas to live in the cities of Tulsa and Oklahoma City.

The roots of many of the state's Hispanic citizens can be traced to those who arrived in the 19th century as workers on the railroads, ranches, and in coal mines. During the Depression, many Latinos labored in cotton fields, but machines phased out those jobs not long after. Today, most first- and second-generation Latinos live in the state's largest cities. Hispanics are the fastest-growing group within the state, more than doubling in population between 1990 and 2000. Other Oklahoma residents claim European or Asian heritage—and many of their ancestors came during the 19th century.

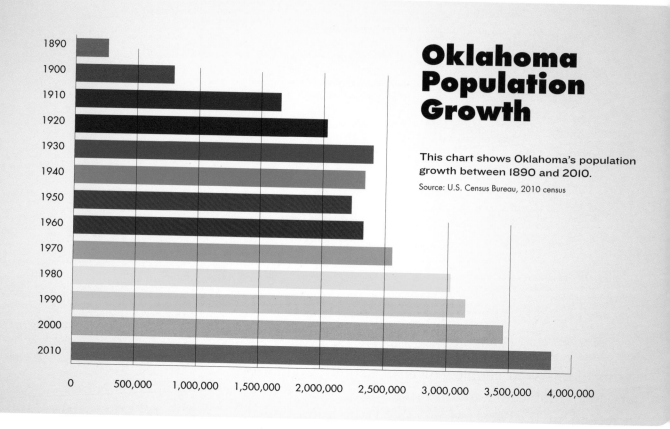

# Oklahoma Population Growth

This chart shows Oklahoma's population growth between 1890 and 2010.

Source: U.S. Census Bureau, 2010 census

# Big City Life

This list shows the population of Oklahoma's biggest cities.

**Oklahoma City** . . . . . . .579,999
**Tulsa**. . . . . . . . . . . . . . .391,906
**Norman** . . . . . . . . . . . .110,925
**Broken Arrow** . . . . . . . .98,850
**Lawton**. . . . . . . . . . . . . .96,867

Source: U.S. Census Bureau, 2010 census

Most Oklahomans live in the urban areas of the eastern portion of the state. The largest cities are the capital, Oklahoma City, and Tulsa. The next three biggest are Norman, Broken Arrow, and Lawton. Like generations before them, many people living in the more rural areas of the state continue to farm and ranch.

## OKLAHOMA EDUCATION

Students in Oklahoma are required to attend school from ages 5 to 18. The state also boasts a strong pre-K program for 4-year-olds. There are currently more than 666,000 school-age kids in Oklahoma. Most attend

# Where Oklahomans Live

The colors on this map indicate population density throughout the state.
The darker the color, the more people live there.

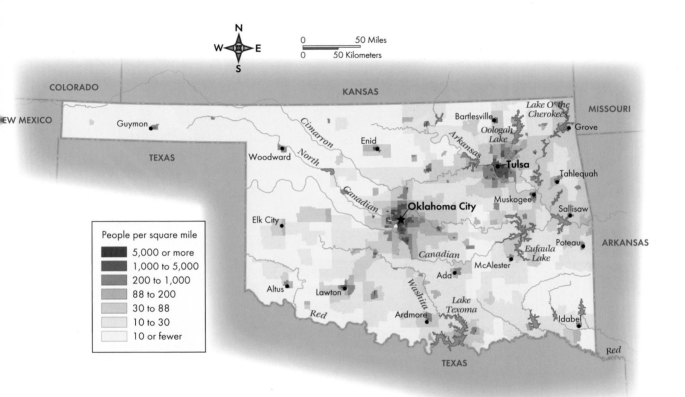

public schools, but there are also 96 accredited private schools in the state.

The Oklahoma Department of Transportation worked with state schools to develop the Safe Route to School Program. This program encourages students to walk or bike to school, and it ensures that these students travel back and forth to school safely. The program promotes healthy habits and cuts down on fuel usage.

Students holding flags from 110 countries take part in the University of Oklahoma graduation in 2004.

The state is home to dozens of colleges and universities. The University of Oklahoma has campuses in Norman and Tulsa, as well as its Health Science Center in Oklahoma City, which prepares students for medical careers. The University of Tulsa was founded in 1894 and has nationally recognized English and psychology departments. Other colleges include Oklahoma State University in Stillwater, Northern Oklahoma College in Tonkawa, Eastern Oklahoma State College in Wilburton, and Western Oklahoma State College in Altus.

In 1990, the Native American Language Act was passed, requiring the United States to preserve, protect, and promote the freedom and rights of all Native Americans to practice, use, and develop their own languages. The University of Oklahoma offers courses in four different Native American languages: Cherokee, Choctaw, Kiowa, and Creek-Seminole. Thousands of Native Americans in the state continue to speak their native tongues today.

## OKLAHOMANS IN SPACE

Oklahoma has produced more astronauts than any other state in the country! It has raised seven of them: Gordon Cooper (the first American to fly two orbits around Earth in a *Mercury* capsule), Shannon Lucid, Thomas Stafford, Stuart Roosa, Owen Garriott, William Pogue, and John Herrington.

A carving found in an ancient mound, part of the Native American culture that is preserved in Oklahoma today

**MINI-BIO**

### SHANNON LUCID: INTERNATIONAL SPACE STATION RECORD HOLDER

Shannon Lucid (1943—) was born in China but grew up in the city of Bethany. She became a biochemist in college. In 1979, she was selected to become an astronaut. She went on four space missions, and then in 1996, she rode the space shuttle *Atlantis* to the Russian space station *Mir*. She stayed on *Mir* for 188 days and four hours—longer than any other American. During that time, she traveled 75.2 million miles (121 million km)!

**? Want to know more?** Visit www.factsfornow.scholastic.com and enter the keyword **Oklahoma**.

## HOW TO TALK LIKE AN OKLAHOMAN

In Oklahoma, you'll hear some unique terminology that you might not find anywhere else in the country. Here are some special words and phrases:

*critter:* creature
*a-goin':* going
*wrassle:* wrestle
*skift:* preparing to do something
*sparkin':* dating
*bumfuzzled:* confused

## HOW TO EAT LIKE AN OKLAHOMAN

A typical meal in Oklahoma is based on traditional southern cooking. Barbecued and fried are two of the most popular ways to prepare meat. And with the state's history of cattle ranching, beef is definitely the meat of choice. Following an Oklahoma dinner, it is hard to imagine that anyone might leave the table hungry—especially when you see what's for dessert!

In Oklahoma, barbecued and grilled foods are popular.

# MENU

## WHAT'S ON THE MENU IN OKLAHOMA?

★ ★ ★

### Chicken fried steak
Part of the state's official meal, this is beef that is dipped in batter, fried, and served up with gravy.

### Barbecued meats
Beef and pork are the favorites, right off the grill.

### Succotash
This is a stew made of corn and beans, staples of the early Native American diet.

### Hot biscuits
Enjoy them from the oven and topped with melting butter.

### Green beans
These are made the traditional southern way, slow-cooked with bacon, of course.

### Fried okra
This slippery vegetable is coated in crunchy batter and deep-fried.

### Pickled cucumbers
They are sour, salty, and snappy.

### Pie
You'll find strawberry or huckleberry, if you are in the Ozarks; peach, if you are in central Oklahoma; wild sand plum, if you are in the west; and pecan, if you are anywhere in the state.

### TRY THIS RECIPE
### Pecan Pie
What's better than homemade pie after a great meal? This delicious recipe can be made with Oklahoma pecans. Be sure to have an adult nearby to help.

**Ingredients:**
½ cup butter
¾ cup light corn syrup
¼ cup honey
1 cup sugar
3 large eggs
1 teaspoon vanilla
⅛ teaspoon salt
1 cup chopped pecans
9-inch pie shell, unbaked
Whipped cream for topping, optional

Pecan pie

**Instructions:**
1. Preheat the oven to 425°F.
2. In a medium saucepan over low to medium heat, cook the butter for 5 to 8 minutes, until it is melted and lightly browned. Pour the butter into a bowl and set it aside.
3. In another saucepan over low heat, combine the corn syrup, honey, sugar, eggs, vanilla, and salt. Stir until smooth. Add the reserved butter and stir again until completely blended.
4. Place the pecans in the pie shell.
5. Pour the mixture over the pecans.
6. Bake at 425°F for 10 minutes, then lower the heat to 325°F and bake another 40 minutes.
7. Allow to cool before serving. Add whipped cream to the top, if you like.

Allan Houser is an award-winning sculptor whose works are seen throughout the state.

## OKLAHOMA ARTS

Oklahoma has a rich arts culture. Public schools offer art classes in the curriculum. And the Oklahoma Arts Institute is an annual program that provides arts training to students ages 14 to 18. There are classes in drawing, sculpture, photography, acting, dance, and poetry, among others.

The state has been home to many talented artists. Among them is Allan Houser (1914–1994), one of the best-known Native American sculptors in the United States. He grew up on a farm near Apache. His sculptures are made from stone, marble, limestone, clay, plaster, steel, and other materials. Houser's works explore subjects relating to his Chiricahua Apache heritage, such as courageous warriors, mothers with children, and ceremonial dancers. One of his pieces, *As Long as the Waters Flow*, stands in front of the capitol in Oklahoma City. Another, *Sacred Rain Arrow,* is at the entrance to the Gilcrease Museum in Tulsa.

One of Oklahoma's most beloved artists is Charles Banks Wilson. Outside of Oklahoma, he is best known for many portraits of Native Americans. Within the state, people visit the state capitol to see his portraits of famous Oklahomans hanging on the walls and four giant murals depicting Oklahoma history in the building's dome.

## Literature

Oklahoma has produced a number of talented writers. Bill Wallace, a former teacher from Chickasha, is known for his books about animals. *Beauty* tells the story of a boy who moves to an Oklahoma farm and forms a close bond with a horse. Wilson Rawls of Scraper wrote the children's classic *Where the Red Fern Grows*, a story about an Ozark Mountain boy and his dogs set during the Great Depression. Vera Cleaver and Hugo native Bill Cleaver cowrote *Where the Lilies Bloom,* a beloved teen novel about the 14-year-old daughter of an Appalachian sharecropper who struggles to keep her siblings together after their father dies.

Author N. Scott Momaday was born in Lawton and spent the first year of his life on a Native American reservation. He was raised in Arizona, where he was taught about his family's Kiowa traditions, as well as the Navajo, Apache, and Pueblo Indian cultures. His first novel, *House Made of Dawn*, which tells of a man's

## S. E. HINTON: TEENAGE AUTHOR

Many high school students recognize the name S. E. (Susan Eloise) Hinton (1948–). She is the author of *The Outsiders*, one of the most popular contemporary novels taught—and sometimes banned—in American English classes. The story follows a 14-year-old boy and his friends as they clash with a rival group of teens. Born in Tulsa, Hinton was only a college freshman in 1967 when the book was published. Today, it is the second-best-selling young adult novel in publishing history. Hinton has also written many other award-winning teen novels.

**? Want to know more?** Visit www.factsfornow.scholastic.com and enter the keyword **Oklahoma**.

struggles to reconnect with his family and heritage after returning from fighting in World War II, won the Pulitzer Prize for Fiction in 1969. He was the first Native American to win the Pulitzer.

Lance Henson is a Native American writer who grew up in a Southern Cheyenne culture on a farm near Calumet. His poems and plays have received acclaim throughout the United States and the world. His works draw upon his knowledge and experience with the Cheyenne culture and language that surrounded him throughout his life in Oklahoma.

## Music

With its strong traditions in cowboy and western culture, it's no surprise that Oklahoma has been the birthplace of many country music superstars. Reba McEntire broke into the music scene in the late 1970s. Born in McAlester, she has produced more than 25

Reba McEntire is a country music superstar from McAlester.

albums, sold 60 million records, won multiple awards—including the prestigious Grammy—and has been dubbed the Queen of Country Music. Singer, songwriter, and guitarist Vince Gill was born in Norman. He was inducted into the Western Performers Hall of Fame at the National Cowboy and Western Heritage Museum in Oklahoma City.

Toby Keith, born in Clinton, is a relative newcomer to the country music scene. He has created a huge fan base all over the world and has collaborated with greats such as Willie Nelson. Tulsa-native Garth Brooks is a Grammy Award winner. He has also received 16 American Music Awards and 11 Country Music Awards. He has sold more than 115 million albums in the United States alone. Checotah-raised Carrie Underwood gained national recognition when she won the *American Idol* title in 2005. She has won two Grammy Awards, one American Music Award, and eight Billboard Music Awards.

But Oklahoma's music isn't all country and western. Jazz guitarist Charlie Christian grew up in Oklahoma City. He is credited with helping develop the styles of bebop, cool jazz, and modern jazz. Opera star Leona Mitchell grew up in Enid before studying music at Oklahoma City University. She later sang with the Metropolitan Opera in New York City and starred in many productions in Europe.

**MINI-BIO**

## RALPH ELLISON: AWARD-WINNING AUTHOR

Born in Oklahoma City, Ralph Ellison (1914–1994) once said, "Literature is colorblind." His novel *The Invisible Man* was published in 1952 and won the National Book Award. The book remains an incredible depiction of a young black man's struggle to find out who he really is. Ellison was working on a trilogy titled *Juneteenth* when he died. *Juneteenth* is a yearly commemoration of the end of slavery in the United States.

**? Want to know more?** Visit www.factsfornow .scholastic.com and enter the keyword **Oklahoma**.

## PUTTING THE ELECTRIC IN THE ELECTRIC GUITAR

Bob Dunn was a musician born in 1908 in Fort Gibson. According to legend, to get more sound out of his instrument, he hooked it up to a car battery at an outdoor dance. His first use of an electric guitar was on a recording made in 1935.

## WILL ROGERS: BELOVED NATIONAL FIGURE

Will Rogers (1879–1935) was an Indian turned cowboy. He learned complicated roping skills, earning him a spot in the *Guinness Book of World Records*. He performed in Wild West shows, where he began telling jokes between his tricks. Soon he was known more for these comments than anything else. Rogers starred in 71 movies, was friends with multiple presidents, and was well known for the phrase "I never met a man I didn't like."

**? Want to know more?** Visit www.factsfornow .scholastic.com and enter the keyword **Oklahoma**.

## Movies

Oklahoma's tumultuous history, terrifying tornadoes, and class differences are all great subjects for moviemakers. The 1940s hits *Red River*, *Cimarron*, and *Oklahoma* were all made there. In addition, Oklahoma was the setting for more recent films, including *Eight Seconds*, *Twister*, *Rain Man*, *The Outsiders*, *Near Dark*, *Far and Away*, *Phenomenon*, and *Elizabethtown*. In 2005, filmmakers from Walt Disney Pictures and Pixar Animation Studios stopped by the Route 66 Rock Café in Stroud. They talked to owner Dawn Welch, and she later became the inspiration for the character of Sally, the blue Porsche in the movie *Cars*.

Oklahoma has also been the home of several talented actors and actresses, including Brad Pitt, Chuck Norris, Tony Randall, Ron Howard, and Alfre Woodard. One of the most beloved personalities in Oklahoma history was Will Rogers, a world-famous comedian, humorist, social commentator, and actor.

The movie *Twister*, starring Bill Paxton and Helen Hunt, was filmed in Oklahoma.

## SOONER STATE SPORTS

Oklahomans are passionate about sports. They went wild in 2012 when the Oklahoma City Thunder, the state's only major league sports team, made it to the National Basketball Association finals. College sports are also big. The University of Oklahoma Sooners have earned 27 national titles in various sports. The football team has won the national title seven times, most recently in 2000. The women's softball team won the national championship in 2013. The men's gymnastics team is a powerhouse, earning national honors eight times, most recently in 2008. The Sooners have also won national titles in baseball, golf, and wrestling.

The Cowboys and Cowgirls of Oklahoma State University have won a combined 51 national titles. That's the fourth-highest record of all colleges in the United States. Of that total, 34 titles have been earned in wrestling. In 2006, the men's golf team won its 10th national championship. The university also boasts national titles in baseball, cross country running, and men's basketball.

Members of the University of Oklahoma Sooners softball team celebrate a victory in 2013.

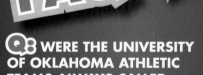

FAQ

**Q8 WERE THE UNIVERSITY OF OKLAHOMA ATHLETIC TEAMS ALWAYS CALLED SOONERS?**

**A8** No. For several years, they were called Rough Riders or Boomers. The Sooner name became official in 1908.

## JIM THORPE: THE WORLD'S GREATEST ATHLETE

While Oklahoma has been home to some of the most gifted athletes in the world, few have been as multitalented as Jim Thorpe (1887–1953). Thorpe was born on the Sauk and Fox Reservation near what is now the town of Prague. He was also part Potawatomi. He played football at the Carlisle Indian School in Pennsylvania and was named an All-American in 1911 and 1912. Also in 1912, he was a member of the U.S. track-and-field team at the Olympic Games in Stockholm, Sweden. He won eight medals, including gold in the **decathlon** and **pentathlon**.

As a professional, Thorpe played football for the Canton Bulldogs, the Cleveland Indians, and the New York Giants, among others. He also played baseball for the New York Giants, the Cincinnati Reds, and the Boston Braves.

**? Want to know more?** Visit www.factsfornow.scholastic.com and enter the keyword **Oklahoma**.

## WORDS TO KNOW

**decathlon** *an athletic contest of ten different track-and-field events*

**pentathlon** *an athletic contest of five different track-and-field events*

Oklahoma native Mickey Mantle played for the New York Yankees from 1951 to 1968.

The University of Tulsa Golden Hurricanes sponsor 18 sports teams. They have captured six national titles—four in women's golf and two in men's basketball. And Chicago Bears football head coach Lovie Smith is a graduate of the University of Tulsa.

Oklahoma has produced some great athletes. Three players from the Sooner State have won the Heisman Trophy for being the year's best college football player: Billy Vessels (1952), Steven Owens (1969), and Billy Sims (1978). Vessels went on to play for the Baltimore Colts as the second overall pick in the NFL draft in 1953. Owens is the Oklahoma Sooners' all-time leading scorer, with 55 touchdowns, and is third on its career-rushing chart with 4,041 yards. Sims led the Oklahoma Sooners to two consecutive Orange Bowl titles in three straight appearances.

Baseball Hall of Famers Mickey Mantle and Johnny Bench both got their start in Oklahoma. A true baseball legend, Mantle was born in Spavinaw and was an all-around athlete at Commerce High School. He played his entire 18-year major league professional career for the New York Yankees, winning three American League MVP

Rodeo star
Jim Shoulders

## BLAKE GRIFFIN: SLAM DUNK CHAMPION

Born on March 16, 1989, in Oklahoma City, Blake Griffin began playing basketball at a young age. By the time he started high school in 2003, he had become well-known locally for his skills on the court.

After two stunning seasons playing college basketball for the University of Oklahoma, Griffin was drafted by the Los Angeles Clippers in 2009. While a knee injury kept him off the court for a full year, he quickly emerged as one of the league's biggest stars after his debut in the 2010-2011 season. He is especially famous for his thunderous slam dunks. He even won the 2011 NBA Slam Dunk Contest by dunking over the top of a car. In 2013, Griffin and his family established a charity to aid victims of the tornado that devastated their home state.

**? Want to know more?** Visit www.factsfornow.scholastic.com and enter the keyword **Oklahoma**.

titles and playing on 16 All-Star teams. During Mantle's years with the Yankees, the team went to the World Series 12 times. Hall of Famer Johnny Bench played for the Cincinnati Reds from 1967 to 1983 and is widely regarded as one of the greatest catchers in Major League Baseball history. He was part of the "Big Red Machine," the nickname given to the Reds when the team dominated the National League from 1972 to 1976. Over that span, they won five division titles, three National League pennants, and two World Series.

Other great sports figures from Oklahoma include boxer Tommy Morrison, golfer Nancy Lopez, rodeo champ Jim Shoulders, and gymnasts Shannon Miller and Bart Conner. These superstars share something with all Sooners—they know that Oklahoma is a great place to live, work, and play.

## READ ABOUT

Governor Mary
Fallin greets
Senator Brian
Bingman at a
special legislative
session on
September
3, 2013.

# CHAPTER SEVEN

# GOVERNMENT

★

C AN YOUNG PEOPLE INFLUENCE THEIR STATE GOVERNMENT? You bet! In 1997, the Oklahoma state legislature approved a bill making the bullfrog the state amphibian. Who came up with the idea? It was seventh-grade students at Brushy Creek School in Sallisaw. Five years later, 11-year-old Daniel Howard realized that there was no state beverage. As a 4-H member in Guthrie whose family owned a dairy farm, he lobbied for milk and succeeded! All of these changes came about because young people saw room for improvement—and worked hard to fill it.

# Capitol Facts

Here are some fascinating facts about Oklahoma's state capitol.

**Designed by** . . . . . . . . . . . Solomon Andrew Layton
and Wemyss Smith
**Ground broken** . . . . . . . . . . . . . . . . June 10, 1914
**Construction began** . . . . . . . . . . . August 4, 1915
**Exterior** . . . . . . . . . . . . . . . . Indiana limestone
**Base** . . . . . . . . . . . . . . . . . . . . . . Black granite
**Floors** . . . . . . . . . . . . . . . . . . . Alabama marble
**Opened** . . . . . . . . . . . . . . . . . . . . June 30, 1917
**Dome dedicated** . . . . . . . . . . November 16, 2002
**Portraits in rotunda** . . . . . . Robert S. Kerr, Sequoyah,
Will Rogers, and Jim Thorpe

## THE CENTER OF GOVERNMENT

Oklahoma's first capitol was in Guthrie, the territorial capital. By the time Oklahoma became a state in 1907, Oklahoma City was where people and businesses were centered. The city petitioned to become the new state capital. A popular vote was held, and Oklahoma City won. Construction on the capitol began at NE 23rd Street and Lincoln Boulevard in 1915.

# Capital City

This map shows places of interest in Oklahoma City, Oklahoma's capital city.

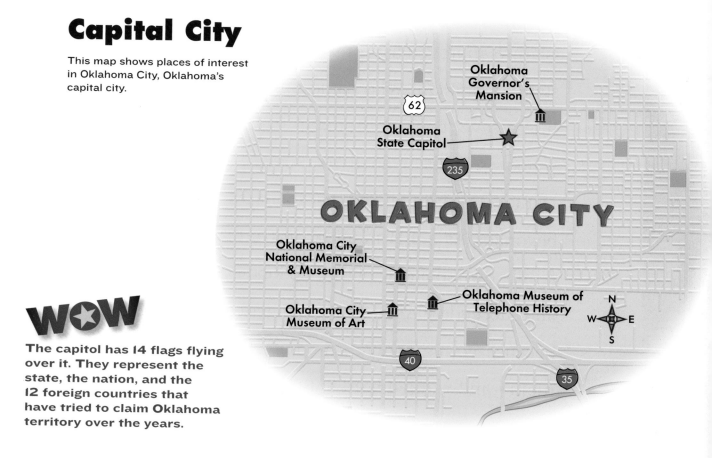

**WOW**

The capitol has 14 flags flying over it. They represent the state, the nation, and the 12 foreign countries that have tried to claim Oklahoma territory over the years.

## A LOOK INSIDE THE DOME

When the original capitol was built in Oklahoma City, it had no dome, which was unusual for such a building. The designer had planned on one, but World War I created shortages of steel and other materials, and a dome was considered a frivolous expense.

Later, when the state decided to add a dome to the building, securing the necessary money was only part of the process. Engineers also had to make sure that the building could withstand the additional weight of a dome. They had to conduct wind tests, since the state is known for its tornadoes. At last, in 2002, the dome was added at a cost of more than $20 million. It is 155 feet (47 m) high and made out of 9,000 individual pieces of stained glass and a mile's worth of lead. On the top sits a 22-foot (7 m) bronze Native American figure called *The Guardian*, chosen after a statewide competition.

## OIL ANYWHERE AND EVERYWHERE

In 1928, oilman and future governor E. W. Marland suspected there was oil under the grounds of the state capitol and governor's mansion. He ordered wells to be drilled there. The people objected. There were rules against this. Marland ignored them and called out the state militia to drill the wells. Oil was found in one of the wells, which was then named Petunia #1 after the flower bed under which it was located.

**The state capitol in Oklahoma City**

## MINI-BIO

### WILLIAM MURRAY: "ALFALFA BILL"

Born in Texas, William Murray (1869–1956) was a colorful politician in Oklahoma history. Married to a Chickasaw woman, he became governor in 1932. Later, he ran for president on a platform of "Bread, Butter, Bacon and Beans." He earned the nickname "Alfalfa" for giving speeches about farming while standing in an alfalfa field. During the Great Depression, he was so devoted to solving the problems of unemployment, poverty, and failing businesses that he donated part of his salary to help feed the needy.

**? Want to know more?** Visit www.factsfornow .scholastic.com and enter the keyword **Oklahoma**.

Surrounding the base of the dome is a series of four murals by artist Charles Banks Wilson. Each panel depicts a period or event in Oklahoma's history. They are titled *Discovery and Exploration*, *Frontier Trade*, *Indian Immigration*, and *Non-Indian Settlement*. Each section is 13 feet (4 m) high and 26 feet (8 m) wide. To make sure that his paintings were completely accurate, Wilson went to the four sites he painted. He used real people as models, first sketching them and then building clay models. Finally, he painted the figures on canvas.

*Discovery and Exploration*, by Charles Banks Wilson, is one of the murals inside the Oklahoma capitol dome.

## HOW THE GOVERNMENT WORKS

Legislators and educators watch as Governor Mary Fallin signs a bill into law in 2011.

When Oklahoma became a state in 1907, it adopted a state constitution. This document outlines the laws and principles that are important to the state. It addresses voting rights, taxes, land for schools, and other issues that are part of running a state. Like other state constitutions, Oklahoma's calls for three branches of government: the executive, the legislative, and the judicial. The state's constitution also contains a bill of rights like the one in the U.S. Constitution. According to Oklahoma's bill of rights, voters in the state can ask the government to make amendments, or changes, to the constitution.

## THE EXECUTIVE BRANCH

The executive branch consists of seven main positions: governor, lieutenant governor, attorney general, secretary of state, treasurer, superintendent of public instruction, and auditor/inspector. The governor, who is elected by the people every four years, appoints other members of the executive branch. They specialize in departments such as corrections (jails and prisons), education (schools),

# Oklahoma's State Government

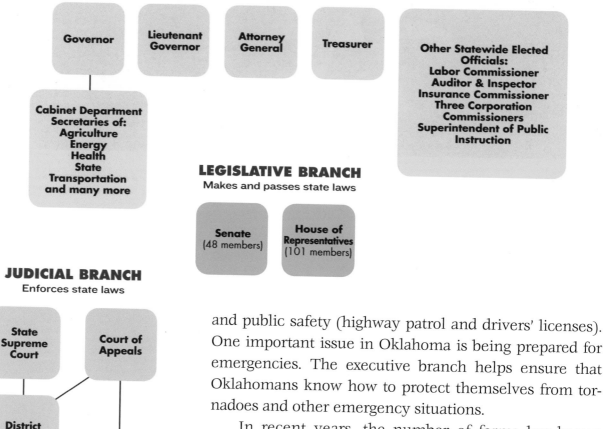

**EXECUTIVE BRANCH**
Carries out state laws

Governor

Lieutenant Governor

Attorney General

Treasurer

Other Statewide Elected Officials:
Labor Commissioner
Auditor & Inspector
Insurance Commissioner
Three Corporation Commissioners
Superintendent of Public Instruction

Cabinet Department Secretaries of:
Agriculture
Energy
Health
State
Transportation
and many more

**LEGISLATIVE BRANCH**
Makes and passes state laws

Senate
(48 members)

House of Representatives
(101 members)

**JUDICIAL BRANCH**
Enforces state laws

State Supreme Court

Court of Appeals

District Courts

Municipal Courts

Municipal Criminal Courts

and public safety (highway patrol and drivers' licenses). One important issue in Oklahoma is being prepared for emergencies. The executive branch helps ensure that Oklahomans know how to protect themselves from tornadoes and other emergency situations.

In recent years, the number of farms has begun to decline. Farming is a demanding life, and often the hard work does not pay off in profits. In 2006, the state adopted a program that may help. Governor Brad Henry signed the Farm-to-School Act, which focuses on getting more state-grown fruits and vegetables into the state's school cafeterias, as well as on educating students about the importance of farming. Field trips to farms, school gardening projects, and cooking demonstrations all help students learn the value of keeping local farms going.

## THE LEGISLATIVE BRANCH

The legislative branch is divided into the senate and the house of representatives. These two bodies meet in the state capitol. The senate is made up of 48 members, and the house has 101 members. These legislators help make laws. But the people of Oklahoma can propose laws. They also tell their leaders how to vote when new laws are being debated.

## THE JUDICIAL BRANCH

The judicial branch is made of judges and courts. The members of this branch help interpret the laws. Judges in cities and towns listen to cases on the local level. They help run the courtroom while cases are being tried. If someone objects to the ruling in a court case, an appeals court will hear the case. Sometimes an appeals court agrees

Legislators gather for a joint session of the Oklahoma house and senate in February 2013.

## REPRESENTING OKLAHOMA

This list shows the number of elected officials who represent Oklahoma, both on the state and national levels.

| Office | Number | Length of Term |
| --- | --- | --- |
| State representatives | 101 | 2 years |
| State senators | 48 | 4 years |
| U.S. representatives | 5 | 2 years |
| U.S. senators | 2 | 6 years |
| Presidential electors | 7 | — |

## MARY FALLIN: A WOMAN IN CHARGE

In 2010, Mary Fallin made history when she was elected the first female governor in Oklahoma history. Before embarking on a political career, Fallin worked for many years as the manager of a chain of hotels. In 1990, she successfully ran for a seat in the Oklahoma House of Representatives. Four years later, she became the first woman ever elected the state's lieutenant governor.

Fallin has focused heavily on creating jobs for Oklahoma's unemployed people. "I love Oklahoma," she has said, "and that's why I'm determined to move this state forward."

**? Want to know more?** Visit www.factsfornow.scholastic.com and enter the keyword **Oklahoma**.

with the first ruling. But sometimes the original ruling may be overturned. The state supreme court hears the appeals of cases already decided in lower courts. This court is made of nine judges.

James Winchester was appoint-ed to the state supreme court in 2000 and was elected chief justice in 2007. He was a district judge for Caddo County and served as a federal judge. While in these positions, he heard a wide range of cases. And he helped establish a program called Children Coping with Divorce.

## INSIDE THE GOVERNOR'S MANSION

For the first two decades after Oklahoma became a state, its governors lived either in their own homes or in hotels, because there was no governor's mansion. Before there was a place built for him, governor Henry Simpson Johnson (1927–1929) waited for the mansion's construction. A spot had been picked out, but the funds were lacking. In 1927, thanks to the growing oil boom (including a gusher right on the south lawn of the capitol), the money came through. By late 1928, the house was finished. It had 19 rooms, including a library, a parlor, a dining room, a ballroom, and a sun-room. Today, it has been modified to 12 rooms.

When Governor William Murray lived in the house in the 1930s, he often let the grass in the yard grow knee-high. Since it was the Depression, he brought in mules to plow the yard, changing it into a vegetable garden so that people could plant potatoes there. During the 1930s and 1940s, oil **derricks** were scattered across the grounds to extract the oil underneath.

In 1995, a major makeover of the mansion began. The state's citizens were asked to donate gifts and their time. They gave more than 1,500 **heirlooms**. Today, the mansion includes an Oklahoma-shaped pool, with the Panhandle portion being a hot tub!

## TRIBAL GOVERNMENT

Oklahoma's cities and counties have their own local governments. But Oklahoma is different from most other states. There are 39 Indian nations based in the state, each with a formal system of tribal government. Native Americans in Oklahoma not only have rights and responsibilities under the U.S. and state

Newly elected Cherokee principal chief Bill John Baker celebrates with his wife, Sherry Robertson-Baker, in October 2011.

A group of adults and students in Guthrie march to support a proposal to improve bridges and roads that are used by school buses.

governments, but they also have them under their own individual tribes. Most of the tribal governments have adopted a three-branch system like the state structure. A chief often serves as the executive, and a tribal council acts as the legislature. Judicial work is done through a tribal court system.

## GOVERNMENT OF THE PEOPLE

Throughout Oklahoma, you'll see citizens helping to make the government run. In towns and cities of all sizes, councils and courts keep their communities safe.

# Oklahoma Counties

This map shows the 77 counties in Oklahoma. Oklahoma City, the state capital, is indicated with a star.

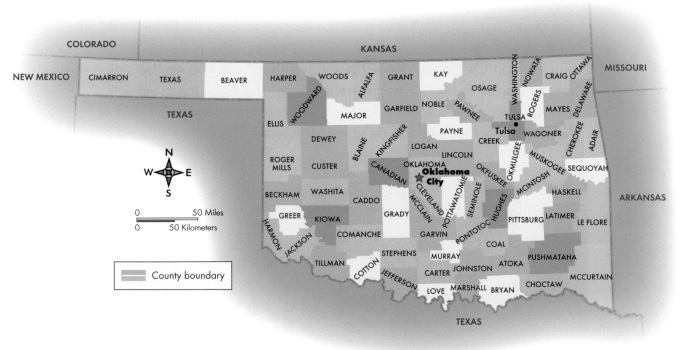

Concerned parents elect people they trust to school boards. The board members vote on school budgets and other proposals. Citizens suggest laws about bicycle safety, better nutrition, highway improvements, and smoking restrictions. County clinics provide vaccines and checkups for kids. The leaders of Oklahoma's government have important jobs to do. But the people of Oklahoma do their part to make the state a safe and secure place to live.

**Oklahoma's Cimarron County, in the Panhandle, is bordered by four states—Texas, New Mexico, Colorado, and Kansas. That's more than any other U.S. county.**

# State Flag

In 1907, Oklahoma was admitted as the 46th state in the Union. The flag adopted by the legislature in 1911 displayed the number 46 at the center of the five-pointed star. The flag Oklahoma flies today—its 14th state flag—was adopted in 1925. At the center is the buckskin shield of an Osage warrior. Crossing the shield are two symbols of peace—an olive branch and a peace pipe. The small tan crosses represent stars, which stand for high ideals and endeavors. The blue field stands for loyalty and devotion. The word *Oklahoma* was added in 1941.

# State Seal

At the center of the great seal of the state of Oklahoma is a five-pointed star with a circle inside it. Inside the circle are three figures: the Frontiersman, the Indian, and Justice. Above the figures is the state motto: *Labor omnia vincit,* which in Latin means "Labor Conquers All Things."

In the upper left point of the star is the symbol of the Cherokee Nation, a small star with a wreath of oak leaves. In the center point is the seal of the Chickasaw Nation, an Indian warrior with bow and shield. The upper right point shows a tomahawk, bow, and three crossed arrows, the emblem of the Choctaw Nation. The symbols in the lower right point represent the Seminole Nation: a house and a factory beside a lake and an Indian in a canoe. The sheaf of wheat and the plow in the lower left point represent the Creek Nation. The stars surrounding the central star represent the states that were in the Union in 1907, when Oklahoma became the 46th state and the seal was adopted. The central star repre-sents Oklahoma.

## READ ABOUT

Raising cattle is
still big business in
Oklahoma.

# CHAPTER EIGHT

# ECONOMY

★

**Y**OU CAN TELL FROM OKLAHOMA'S MOTTO "LABOR CONQUERS ALL THINGS" THAT SOONERS BELIEVE IN HARD WORK. Even during the most difficult years of the Depression and the Dust Bowl, most people stayed in their home state and made sure their families survived. Their persistence paid off. Oil production helped the state flourish. Today, Oklahoma also is a leader in cattle production and agriculture.

## SEE IT HERE!

### BRAUM FARM

Stop by Tuttle, a city of fewer than 5,000 people, to see the Braum farm, where more than 10,000 cows are milked three times a day, every single day of the year. The milk is turned into ice cream and other tasty treats for the 280 Braum's Ice Cream and Dairy Stores throughout Oklahoma, Kansas, Texas, Missouri, and Arkansas.

## CATTLE AND AGRICULTURE

Raising cattle has been important to Oklahoma's economy since the days of 19th-century cattle drives. Today, beef production is a major industry for the state. In fact, Oklahoma ranks fourth nationally in the production of cattle.

Workers on an oil rig in Oklahoma

# Major Agricultural and Mining Products

This map shows where Oklahoma's major agricultural and mining products come from. See a pig? That means hogs are raised there.

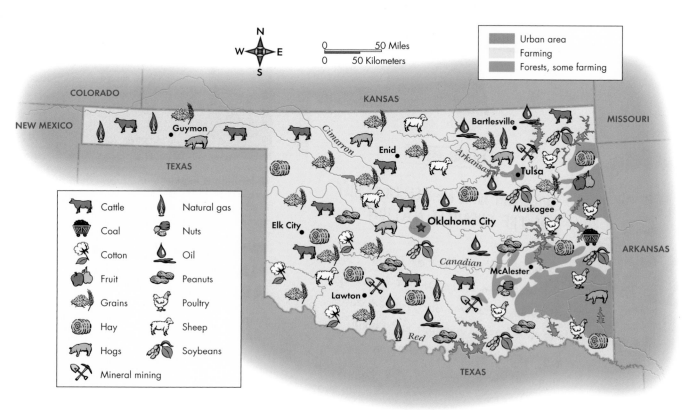

Oklahoma farms grow a variety of crops. Wheat, pecans, peanuts, and peaches are all grown in large quantities. Other crops include cotton, soybeans, and hay. These crops bring a large amount of money to the state.

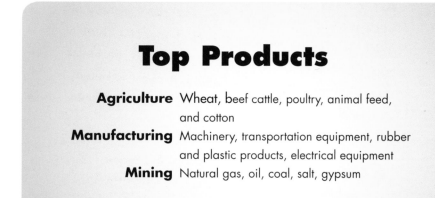

# Top Products

**Agriculture** Wheat, beef cattle, poultry, animal feed, and cotton

**Manufacturing** Machinery, transportation equipment, rubber and plastic products, electrical equipment

**Mining** Natural gas, oil, coal, salt, gypsum

Oklahoma is exploring the production of alternative fuels. Biodiesel , which can be made from vegetable oil, is considered by some to be the fuel of the future.

## MINI-BIO

### WILLIAM WAYNE KEELER: CHIEF OF THE CHEROKEE NATION

William Wayne Keeler (1908–1987) was born in Texas but grew up in Bartlesville, Oklahoma. He studied engineering in college and began working for Phillips Petroleum. During World War II, he served in the Petroleum Administration for War. He also supervised the building of an oil refinery in Mexico. A Cherokee, he was named chief of the Cherokee Nation in 1949. After many years with Phillips Petroleum, Keeler became chief executive officer of the company in 1967. In 1971, he became the first elected chief of the Cherokees since Oklahoma statehood. He began the Cherokee National Holiday and the Cherokee National Historical Society. In 1975, Keeler retired from the position of chief.

**? Want to know more?** Visit www.factsfornow .scholastic.com and enter the keyword **Oklahoma**.

## OIL AND OTHER NATURAL RESOURCES

The 19th-century discovery of black gold (oil) in Oklahoma was a major factor in the state's economy. In fact, the mining of natural resources is Oklahoma's primary industry. As of June 2013, Oklahoma ranked fifth nationally, producing 9,615,000 barrels of oil per year. It also ranks fourth in the production of natural gas. Oklahoma's economy is one of the fastest growing in the nation. The production of oil and natural gas is a key reason for that growth.

The state is also rich in coal deposits, which were discovered in Pittsburg County (in the Choctaw Nation) in the 1870s. Salt is mined in the north-central Great Salt Plain region, and gypsum is found in the Gypsum Hills in western Oklahoma. Other mining products include limestone, red granite, sand, gravel, and clay.

State forests provide a source of hardwood lumber, including oak, hickory, ash, and walnut. These kinds of wood are used for building construction and making furniture.

## THE CORPORATE WORLD

Today, Oklahoma's economy relies on its factories that process foods and minerals. Companies such as Coca-Cola, General Motors, and Goodyear all have operations in the state. The health of these businesses is important to keeping the state economy stable. Prices

## FAQ

**Q: WHAT IS THE MINERAL GYPSUM USED FOR?**

**A:** Gypsum has many uses. You'll find it in sheetrock and plaster, which is used to build walls, and plaster of Paris, which helps make models, casts, and surgical splints. You'll also find it in cement and blackboard chalk.

## THINK ABOUT IT!

## A World Beyond Oil

Oklahoma has relied on the production of oil for more than a century. But finding alternatives to oil is a good idea. Many people believe that exploring the creation and use of **biofuel** is a smart solution. Governor Brad Henry says, "Biofuels are a critical component in reducing the nation's dependence on foreign oil, protecting the environment, creating high-paying jobs and diversifying our state's economy."

Source: Office of Governor Brad Henry. March 12, 2007

### WORD TO KNOW

**biofuel** *an energy source made from plants or plant-derived materials*

Oklahoman Carl McGee came up with the idea of a parking meter to limit the time a person could take up one parking spot. The first one was installed in July 1935.

for oil and cattle can change a lot, so demand goes up and down. But if the other industries in the state remain steady, the fluctuations in oil and cattle are not so worrisome.

Another important business is newspaper publishing. The first newspaper in the area was the *Cherokee Advocate*. This paper was published in both Cherokee and English, and it dates back to 1844. Other historic publications include the *Choctaw Telegraph* (1848), the *Choctaw Intelligencer* (1850), the *Oklahoma Star* (1874), and the *Choctaw Champion* (1883). When Oklahoma became a state in 1907, more than 1,500 newspapers were being published. Today, the *Daily Oklahoman* and *Tulsa World* have the largest readerships in the state.

Oklahoma boasts a number of magazine and book publishers as well. The Oklahoma University Press is headquartered in Norman. It produces books about Native American culture, Western history, political science, and other subjects. Saxon Publishers, also in Norman, publishes mathematics, phonics, and physics books for students in grades kindergarten through 12. PennWell Publishing in Tulsa produces trade magazines and newsletters such as *Oil & Gas Journal*.

## MINI-BIO

## SYLVAN GOLDMAN: GROCERY CART INVENTOR

Sylvan Goldman (1898–1984) may not be a name that many recognize, but his invention is used daily throughout the country. The owner of an Oklahoma City supermarket, he noticed his customers often left when their arms could not hold anything else. To help, he invented the "folding basket carriage"—today's grocery cart. It was far from a success. Goldman couldn't get his customers to use one. They thought it looked too much like a baby carriage. Finally, he hired people of all ages to walk around the store with his cart. It worked! Soon these shopping carts were everywhere.

**?** **Want to know more?** Visit www.factsfornow .scholastic.com and enter the keyword **Oklahoma**.

## INTO THE FUTURE

Other key employers in Oklahoma include schools and the U.S. Postal Service. Military bases such as Fort Sill and Tinker Air Force Base make important contributions to the economy. Some of the nation's largest companies have expanded to Oklahoma's cities in recent years, including Dell and U.S. Cellular. Oklahoma is home to smaller companies, as well. They produce candles, candy, soap, and fabric. Oklahoma's diverse industrial base and hardworking people help keep the state's economy strong.

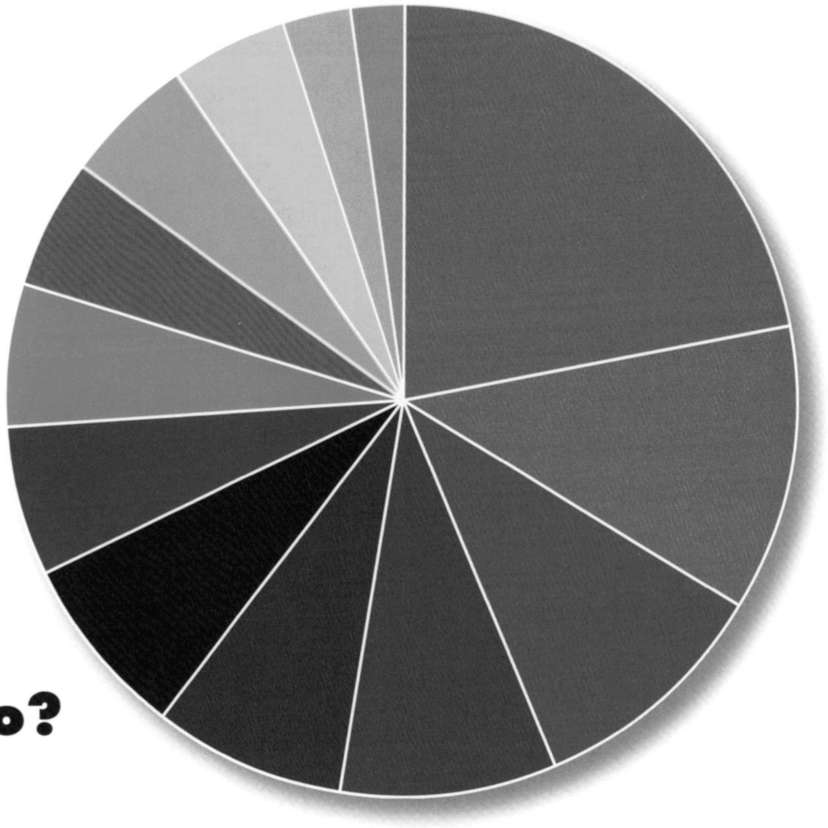

# What Do Oklahomans Do?

**This color-coded chart shows what industries Oklahomans work in.**

**22.2%** Educational services, and health care and social assistance, 374,644

**11.6%** Retail trade, 194,663

**10.0%** Manufacturing, 169,120

**8.7%** Arts, entertainment, and recreation, and accommodation and food services, 146,362

**8.0%** Professional, scientific, and management, and administrative and waste management services, 134,193

**7.3%** Construction, 123,766

**6.2%** Public administration, 103,779

**5.9%** Finance and insurance, and real estate and rental and leasing, 99,971

**5.3%** Transportation and warehousing, and utilities, 89,368

**5.2%** Other services, except public administration, 87,787

**4.6%** Agriculture, forestry, fishing and hunting, and mining, 78,278

**3.0%** Wholesale trade, 50,047

**2.0%** Information, 33,051

Source: U.S. Census Bureau, 2010 census

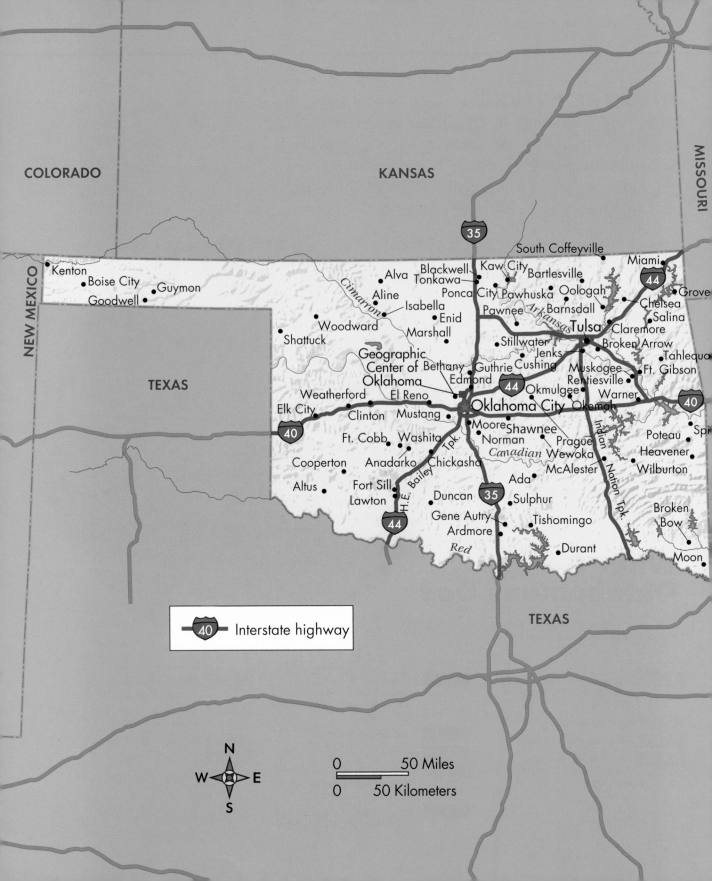

COLORADO

KANSAS

MISSOURI

NEW MEXICO

Kenton
Boise City    Guymon
Goodwell

Blackwell    Kaw City
Alva    Tonkawa                    Bartlesville    South Coffeyville    Miami
Aline                Ponca City    Pawhuska    Oologah    Grove
Isabella        Pawnee        Barnsdall        Chelsea
Enid                    Arkansas        Salina
Woodward    Marshall                Stillwater    Tulsa    Claremore
Shattuck                                Jenks    Broken Arrow
Geographic                        Cushing        Tahlequah
Center of    Bethany    Guthrie            Muskogee    Ft. Gibson
Oklahoma    Edmond            Okmulgee    Rentiesville
Weatherford    El Reno                Oklahoma City    Okemah    Warner
Elk City        Mustang                        Poteau    Spi
Clinton            Moore    Shawnee            Heavener
Ft. Cobb    Washita    Norman    Prague    Wewoka    McAlester    Wilburton
Cooperton    Anadarko    Chickasha    Canadian        Broken
Altus        Fort Sill            Ada        Bow
Lawton            Duncan    Sulphur        Moon
            Gene Autry    Tishomingo
            Ardmore
            Red        Durant

35

44

40

44

40

44

35

44

TEXAS

TEXAS

40  Interstate highway

N
W    E
S

0          50 Miles
0          50 Kilometers

CHAPTER NINE

**TRAVEL GUIDE**

# TRAVEL GUIDE

★

HIKE THROUGH THE WICHITA MOUNTAINS OR THE TALLGRASS PRAIRIE PRESERVE TO GET A GLIMPSE OF OKLAHOMA'S NATURAL BEAUTY. Tour the Red Earth Museum to see authentic artifacts from the area's Native American culture, or visit regional museums to learn about the history of railroads, dolls, or wrestling. Follow the map and see where it takes you.

← Follow along with this travel map. We'll begin in Kaw City and travel all the way down to Broken Bow!

# THE PANHANDLE

**THINGS TO DO:** Climb to the top of Black Mesa, study antique wagons and buggies from the Santa Fe Trail, or take pictures next to dozens of windmills!

## Kenton

★ **Black Mesa State Park and Nature Preserve:** This park in Oklahoma's Panhandle got its name from the layer of black lava rock that coated the mesa about 30 million years ago. The nature preserve is located 15 miles (24 km) from the state park and features Black Mesa, Oklahoma's highest point.

Black Mesa

## Boise City

★ **Cimarron Heritage Center Museum and Information Center:** The museum houses a restored Santa Fe depot and blacksmith shop, a homestead dugout and windmill exhibit, along with antique machinery, wagons and buggies from the Santa Fe Trail, and much more.

## Goodwell

★ **No Man's Land Historical Museum:** Check out a fine selection of artifacts from the William E. Baker archaeological collection, materials from the Native basket maker culture, and geological materials from the region.

## Shattuck

★ **Shattuck Windmill Museum and Park:** This is a display of 46 rare and restored windmills from 1870 to 1970. Some are solid wood or folding wood wheels, and no two are alike. A 5-foot (1.5 m) Star Zephyr, an 18-foot (5.5 m) steel Samson, and an 18-foot (5.5 m) Railroad Eclipse are just a few examples of what you will find here. A great place for picture taking!

# NORTH CENTRAL REGION

**THINGS TO DO: See Native American artifacts and exhibits, tour one of the largest railroad museums in the country, or touch a real dinosaur egg.**

## Kaw City

★ **Kanza Museum:** Check out this museum of the Kaw Indian Nation, with a variety of exhibits on Native American culture and a fossil exhibit.

## Blackwell

★ **Top of Oklahoma Historical Society Museum:** Housed in the 1912 Electric Park Pavilion, this museum contains items dating from the 1893 Cherokee Strip land run to the present. Exhibits cover everything from Native American culture to the Victorian era to Wild West shows.

## Enid

★ **Railroad Museum of Oklahoma:** This museum houses one of the largest collections of railroad material in the United States. Exhibits include more than 900 pieces of dining-car china and silver service from passenger trains of the past, maps depicting various railroad lines, railroad paintings, depot clocks, steam engine bells, locks, keys, and a functioning telegraph system.

★ **Leonardo's Discovery Warehouse & Adventure Quest:** Touch a real dinosaur egg, slide down a three-story slide, build your own castle in the carpentry shop, or get lost in a variety of bridges, tunnels, and mazes. You can also create your own style of music in the music lab, tell time on a sundial, or travel to the moon in a simulated space shuttle.

## Ponca City

★ **Standing Bear Park:** A 22-foot (7 m) bronze sculpture of Ponca chief Standing Bear is the focal point of this park, which also has audio centers honoring the six Native American tribes around Ponca City.

★ **Pioneer Woman Statue and Museum:** This 17-foot (5 m) bronze monument represents the thousands of courageous women who helped forge homes in new lands. The museum is dedicated to the heroic pioneer women who braved danger and hardships to settle Oklahoma.

## Woodward

★ **Fort Supply Historic Site:** Here you can learn about one of the oldest military bases in the state. Original buildings offer insight into how soldiers in Indian Territory lived.

★ **Plains Indians and Pioneers Museum:** This museum helps visitors understand the history of the region through the eyes of both the native Plains Indians and the American pioneers. Tour exhibits on ranching, homesteading, the Dust Bowl, the 1947 tornado, the discovery of oil and gas, and Native American artwork.

## Aline

★ **Sod House Museum:** Visit this furnished sod house to imagine what life was like for Oklahoma's early settlers.

## Pawnee

★ **Pawnee Bill Ranch:** Tour the historic ranch of the legendary Pawnee Bill. You'll see props from his famous Wild West show, with colorful displays of the fancy outfits, boots, guns, saddles, and swords used by Pawnee Bill's performers.

# TULSA REGION

**THINGS TO DO:** Visit the official shrine to Mickey Mantle, hike through the Tallgrass Prairie Preserve, or learn about the Cherokee Nation of Oklahoma.

## Tulsa

★ **Gilcrease Museum:** Offering tours, workshops, and musical events, this museum houses the world's largest, most comprehensive collection of art and artifacts of the American West and an unparalleled collection of Native American art and artifacts.

★ **Philbrook Museum of Art:** This is one of the best art museums in the Great Plains region. View a diverse array of exhibits, including Native American, African, Asian, and European art.

Philbrook Museum of Art

★ **Oklahoma Jazz Hall of Fame:**
This museum houses a music library of video and audio recordings of various artists. Photographs of jazz greats line the walls, and an art gallery completes the museum, with sculptures depicting musical themes and performers.

★ **Tulsa Air and Space Museum and Planetarium:** This museum features rare and vintage aircraft such as Spartan C-2 and C-3 aircraft built in Tulsa during the 1930s, an F-14A Tomcat, Rockwell Ranger 2000, and other locally built aircraft. Interactive exhibits include flight simulators and much more.

## SEE IT HERE!

### MICKEY MANTLE MEMORIAL EXHIBIT AND MUSEUM

If you venture past the town of Grove, take time to stop by the Mickey Mantle Memorial Exhibit and Museum. Here you'll find a huge collection of memorabilia relating to the great New York Yankee and Oklahoma native Mickey Mantle. Exhibits include autographs, photos, balls, bats, gloves, jerseys, caps, and New York Yankees items.

## SEE IT HERE!

### TULSA ZOO

A wildlife adventure of a lifetime! The Tulsa Zoo offers a unique and exciting journey into the natural world. Visitors can see a polar bear from the Arctic or a red kangaroo from Australia. Trek to the tropics in the tropical American rain forest exhibit, where sloths, tamarin monkeys, bats, and poison dart frogs mingle.

### Grove

★ **Har-Ber Village:** Tour this reconstructed turn-of-the-20th-century village featuring artifacts and collections from the area. Visit historic buildings to get a sense of early pioneer construction on the frontier and how people lived.

### Pawhuska

★ **Tallgrass Prairie Preserve:** This diverse grassland and forest is home to more than 300 species of birds. Other wildlife in the preserve includes white-tailed deer, bobcats, armadillos, beavers, woodchucks, badgers, coyotes, and more!

## Barnsdall

★ **Bigheart Museum:** Named after prominent Osage chief James Bigheart, the museum includes Cherokee and Osage artifacts and area history, including the story of how the town name changed from Bigheart to Barnsdall.

## Fort Gibson

★ **Fort Gibson Historic Site and Interpretative Center:** This national historic landmark, the first army post in Indian Territory, was in operation from 1824 to 1890. The site includes 80 acres (32 ha) of grounds, with 29 historic buildings and numerous ruins. Exhibits and living history programs relate to the settlement of Indian Territory and the development of the fort through its 70 years of occupation.

## Jenks

★ **Oklahoma Aquarium:** This aquarium features more than 100 exhibits, eight major galleries, and more than 4,000 creatures from Earth's waters.

### SEE IT HERE!

### HEAVENER RUNESTONE STATE PARK

Close to the small town of Heavener, near the Arkansas border, is a slab of stone that looks almost like an ancient billboard. It is 12 feet (3.7 m) tall, 10 feet (3 m) wide, and 16 inches (41 cm) thick. There is writing on it: eight distinct characters with rounded edges. For centuries, no one knew what the markings meant. In 1923, the Smithsonian Institution stated they were Norse runes, or alphabet symbols, but had no idea what they actually said. In 1967, experts determined that the writing was actually a date: November 11, 1012. In 1970, a state park was constructed around the stone to keep it safe. Efforts to actually date the stone have been going on for decades, and still no one is sure if this stone dates back to 800 CE or is a modern-day hoax.

## Tahlequah

★ **Cherokee Heritage Center:** Learn more about Cherokee history and culture here. Located in the foothills of the Ozark Mountains, the center is home to the Tsa-La-Gi Ancient Village, Adams Corner Rural Village, the Trail of Tears exhibit, and the Cherokee National Museum.

Inside the Woolaroc Museum

## Bartlesville

★ **Woolaroc Museum and Wildlife Preserve:** This natural preserve is home to native species such as the bison, elk, and longhorn cattle. The museum houses a unique selection of western and Native American artifacts and artwork.

## Claremore

★ **Will Rogers Memorial Museum:** Visit the shrine to the legendary American cowboy, Will Rogers. See film and radio highlights and trick ropes and show props used by the legendary performer.

## Ozark Mountains and Plateau

★ Hike through this beautiful scenic land region, which offers plenty of outdoor fun.

## OKLAHOMA CITY REGION

**THINGS TO DO:** Explore the history of photography, learn about the sport of wrestling, or walk through the hallways of Oklahoma's historic capitol.

## Oklahoma City

★ **Oklahoma History Center:** This museum offers more than 2,000 artifacts reflecting Oklahoma's inspiring and adventurous past. Visitors can also take a walking tour of the Red River Valley, noting landforms, vegetation, and important historical locations.

★ **Science Museum Oklahoma:** Visitors here can enjoy hands-on activities, see railroad cars and World War II airplanes, or take a walk in the gardens.

★ **International Photography Hall of Fame and Museum:** This museum is dedicated to the history of photography and highlights some of the world's greatest photographers. It has four large galleries displaying historical and contemporary traveling exhibitions from around the world. The permanent collection features the works of Ansel Adams, Dorothea Lange, Edward Steichen, and many more.

*The End of the Trail* at the National Cowboy and Western Heritage Museum

★ **National Cowboy and Western Heritage Museum:** Dedicated to the legacy of the American cowboy and Western heritage, this complex contains Prosperity Junction, a 14,000-square-foot (1,300 sq m) early 20th-century Western town, and major exhibition galleries such as the American Cowboy Gallery, the American Rodeo Gallery, and the Western Performers Gallery.

★ **Oklahoma State Capitol:** Walk the halls of the historic state capitol and visit the legislative chambers, where important decisions about the state of Oklahoma are made every day. Don't miss the portraits of Robert S. Kerr, Sequoyah, Will Rogers, and Jim Thorpe in the rotunda.

★ **Oklahoma City National Memorial and Museum:** This memorial was created to honor those who were killed, those who survived, and those who were changed forever by the 1995 bombing of the Alfred P. Murrah Federal Building in Oklahoma City. The museum stands as a testimony to the effects of violence, and it promotes peace and hope for the future.

★ **Oklahoma City Zoo and Botanical Garden:** Visit this remarkable zoo, featuring primates, aquatic animals, a unique butterfly garden, and much more.

★ **Red Earth Museum:** This museum features exhibits dedicated to encouraging the preservation of American Indian cultures.

★ **National Softball Hall of Fame and Museum:** Displays depict the colorful history of softball and its greatest players. Various facets of the sport are featured, including fast, slow, and modified pitch; umpires; and youth and championship teams, as well as those players inducted into the hall of fame.

### Guthrie

★ **Oklahoma Sports Museum:**
Check out Oklahoma's official
sports museum. It features a collection of memorabilia honoring athletes who were born, lived, or went
to college in Oklahoma and went
on to be professional, Olympic, or
national champions.

### Stillwater

★ **National Wrestling Hall of Fame
and Museum:** This hall of fame is
devoted to amateur and Olympic
wrestling. Exhibits and displays
include the Honors Court, a Wall
of Champions, and numerous
sculptures, photographs, trophies,
uniforms, and memorabilia.

## SEE IT HERE!

### FRONTIER CITY THEME PARK

Stroll through an authentic 1880s western town, and enjoy
more than 75 rides, shows, games, and attractions. Relive
the famous gunfight at the OK Corral, and catch Frontier
City's six live shows. Ride the exciting roller coasters. Brave
the Renegade Rapids river raft ride, the perilous Time
Warp, and the Mystery River Log Flume.

★ **Oklahoma WONDERtorium:**
Enjoy interactive exhibits designed
to provoke excitement and curi-
osity in the young and young at
heart.

## SOUTHWEST REGION

**THINGS TO DO:** See buffalo
and Texas longhorns, visit
the historic Route 66 Museum, or take in the
culture and heritage of the Great Plains region.

### Lawton

★ **Wichita Mountains Wildlife
Refuge:** Enjoy more than 59,000
acres (23,900 ha) of national
refuge, which is home to buffalo,
Texas longhorn cattle, prairie dogs,
elk, and deer. This site also offers
incredible scenery and views for
hikers and photographers.

★ **Museum of the Great Plains:**
The museum spotlights the cul-
tural and natural history of the
Great Plains of North America. It
also houses an outstanding library
and archives dedicated to the Great
Plains region.

**The Museum of the Great Plains
houses more than 3,200 20th-century
Plains Indians artifacts!**

## Elk City

★ **Farm and Ranch Museum:**
Here you'll find historic farming
equipment and an extensive
collection that includes windmills,
tractors, threshers, and various
early farm tools.

## Clinton

★ **Oklahoma Route 66 Museum:**
This museum showcases all eight
states through which this famous
road extended. Artifacts and antique
cars, along with rare historical documents and collections, recapture the
spirit of Route 66.

## Anadarko

★ **Southern Plains Indian
Museum:** The museum displays
richly varied arts of western
Oklahoma peoples, including
the Kiowas, Comanches, Kiowa-
Apaches, Southern Cheyennes,
Southern Arapahos, Wichitas,
Caddos, Delawares, and Ft. Sill
Apaches. Exhibits include clothing,
shields, weapons, baby carriers,
toys, and much more.

★ **National Hall of Fame for
Famous American Indians:**
You'll see more than 40 bronze
busts of famous American Indians,
including Sequoyah, Captain Black
Beaver, Sitting Bull, Geronimo, and
Pocahontas.

★ **Philomathic Museum:**
Experience the past through the
possessions of pioneer families,
railroad memorabilia, American
Indian dolls, military items, and
photo collections, as well as a re-
created country store and doctor's
office.

# SOUTH-SOUTHEAST REGION

**THINGS TO DO:** Visit a shrine
to a great Western film star, view Native
American artifacts, or see an impressive doll
collection.

## Sulphur

★ **Arbuckle Historical Society
Museum:** What will you see here?
Original beaded clothing of Native
Americans, a loom dating back to
1850, military artifacts, a broom
factory, school picture displays, and
a room displaying home life in pre-
statehood days.

Antique dolls

## Ardmore

★ **Eliza Cruce Hall Doll Museum:**
This is an impressive collection of
300 of the world's finest dolls, with
rare examples of doll makers' art.
The collection of rare and antique
dolls started in 1936, when Hall (the
niece of the state's second governor)
purchased a doll on a trip to Europe.

★ **Military Memorial Museum:**
Visitors here can explore more
than 6,000 square feet (550 sq m)
of military artifacts, dating from
the American Revolution to Desert
Storm and covering all military
branches. There are documents,
photographs, uniforms, weapons,
knives, models, medals, and per-
sonal memorabilia from veterans
from all over the United States.

## Gene Autry

★ **Gene Autry Oklahoma Museum:**
Check out a collection of memorabilia—from his early days to his
movies and music—of Western
movie star and singing legend
Gene Autry.

## Broken Bow

★ **Forest Heritage Center Museum:**
This fascinating museum tells
the story of forestry, including
photo displays of the Civilian
Conservation Corps, a wood art gallery, and a tree trail.

★ **Gardner Mansion and Museum:**
This museum was built in 1884 for
Jefferson Gardner, who went on to
be the chief of the Choctaw. Nearby
are the remains of a 2,000-year-old
cypress tree that was a landmark
to the Choctaws who traveled the
Trail of Tears.

## Idabel

★ **Museum of the Red River:** See
Caddo and Choctaw artifacts, pre-
Columbian objects from Middle
and South America, Native arts
and crafts from throughout the
Americas, and a cast skeleton of
a dinosaur.

An exhibit at the Museum of the Red River

# SCIENCE, TECHNOLOGY, ENGINEERING, & MATH PROJECTS

Make weather maps, graph population statistics, and research endangered species that live in the state.

## 120

# PRIMARY VS. SECONDARY SOURCES

## 121

So what are primary and secondary sources, and what's the diff? This section explains all that and where you can find them.

# BIOGRAPHICAL DICTIONARY

## 133

This at-a-glance guide highlights some of the state's most important and influential people. Visit this section and read about their contributions to the state, the country, and the world.

# RESOURCES

Books and much more. Take a look at these additional sources for information about the state.

## 138

# WRITING PROJECTS

## Create an Election Brochure or Web Site!

★ Run for office! Throughout this book you've read about some of the issues that concern Oklahoma today. As a candidate for governor of Oklahoma, create a campaign brochure or Web site.

★ Explain how you meet the qualifications to be governor of Oklahoma.

★ Talk about the three or four major issues you'll focus on if you're elected. Remember, you'll be responsible for Oklahoma's budget. How would you spend the taxpayers money?

**SEE:** Chapter Seven, pages 87–88.

## State Quarter Project

From 1999 to 2008, the U.S. Mint introduced new quarters commemorating each of the 50 states in the order that they were admitted to the Union. Each quarter features a unique design on its back

**GO TO:** www.factsfornow.scholastic.com. Enter the keyword **Oklahoma** and look for the link to the Oklahoma quarter.

★ Research the significance of the image. Who designed the quarter?

★ Design your own Oklahoma quarter. What images would you choose?

★ Make a poster showing the Oklahoma quarter and label each image.

## Create an interview script with a famous person from Oklahoma!

★ Research various famous Oklahomans, such as Mickey Mantle, Carrie Underwood, Will Rogers, Garth Brooks, Johnny Bench, Wilma Mankiller, Ralph Ellison, and many others.

★ Based on your research, pick one person you would most like to interview.

★ Write a script of the interview. What questions would you ask? How would this famous person answer? Create a question-and-answer format. You may want to supplement this writing project with a recorded voice dramatization of the interview.

**SEE:** Chapter Six, pages 74–81 or the Biographical Dictionary on pages 133–136.

# ART PROJECTS

## Create a PowerPoint Presentation or Visitors' Guide

**Welcome to Oklahoma!**

Oklahoma is a great place to visit and to live! From its natural beauty to its historical sites, there's plenty to see and do. In your PowerPoint presentation or brochure, highlight 10 to 15 of Oklahoma's fascinating landmarks. Be sure to include:

★ a map of the state showing where these sites are located

★ photos, illustrations, Web links, natural history facts, geographic stats, climate and weather, plants, and wildlife, recent discoveries.

**SEE:** Chapter Nine, pages 104–115.

## Illustrate the Lyrics to the Mississippi State Song ("Oklahoma!")

Use markers, paints, photos, collage, colored pencils, or computer graphics to illustrate the lyrics to "Oklahoma!" Turn your illustrations into a picture book, or scan them into a PowerPoint and add music.

**SEE:** The lyrics to "Oklahoma!" on page 128.

## Tell a Visual History

Like the early Native Americans of the Oklahoma region, use painting, sculpture, quilting, or dance to tell the story of your family history.

**SEE:** Chapter Two, pages 24–31.

A Comanche village

# SCIENCE, TECHNOLOGY, ENGINEERING, & MATH PROJECTS

## Graph Population Statistics!

★ Compare population statistics (such as ethnic background, birth, death, and literacy rates) in Oklahoma counties or major cities.

★ In your graph or chart, look at population density and write sentences describing what the population statistics show; graph one set of population statistics and write a paragraph explaining what the graphs reveal.

**SEE:** Chapter Six, pages 66–68.

## Create a Weather Map of Oklahoma!

Use your knowledge of Oklahoma's geography to research and identify conditions that result in specific weather events, including thunderstorms and tornadoes. What is it about the geography of Oklahoma that makes it vulnerable to things such as tornadoes? Create a weather map or poster that shows the weather patterns over the state, or display wet and dry years between 1895 and the present. Include a caption explaining the technology used to measure weather phenomena such as tornadoes, and provide data.

**SEE:** Chapter One, pages 17–19.

## Track Endangered Species

Using your knowledge of Oklahoma's wildlife, research what animals and plants are endangered or threatened.

★ Find out what the state is doing to protect these species.

★ Chart known populations of the animals and plants, and report on changes in certain geographic areas.

**SEE:** Chapter One, page 21, 22–23.

Whooping crane

# PRIMARY VS. SECONDARY SOURCES

## What's the Diff?

**Your teacher may require at least one or two primary sources and one or two secondary sources for your assignment.** So, what's the difference between the two?

★ **Primary sources are original.** You are reading the actual words of someone's diary, journal, letter, autobiography, or interview. Primary sources can also be photographs, maps, prints, cartoons, news/film footage, posters, first-person newspaper articles, drawings, musical scores, and recordings. By the way, when you conduct a survey, interview someone, shoot a video, or take photographs to include in a project, you are creating primary sources!

★ **Secondary sources are what you find in encyclopedias, textbooks, articles, biographies, and almanacs.** These are written by a person or group of people who tell about something that happened to someone else. Secondary sources also recount what another person said or did. This book is an example of a secondary source.

## Now that you know what primary sources are—where can you find them?

★ **Your school or local library:** Check the library catalog for collections of original writings, government documents, musical scores, and so on. Some of this material may be stored on microfilm.

★ **Historical societies:** These organizations keep historical documents, photographs, and other materials. Staff members can help you find what you are looking for. History museums are also great places to see primary sources firsthand.

★ **The Internet:** There are lots of sites that have primary sources you can download and use in a project or assignment.

# TIMELINE

★ ★ ★

## U.S. Events · 1500 · Oklahoma Events

**1541**
Francisco Vásquez de Coronado reaches the region and claims it for Spain.

**1565**
Spanish admiral Pedro Menéndez de Avilés founds St. Augustine, Florida, the oldest continuously occupied European settlement in the continental United States.

**1600**

**1619**
The first African indentured laborers in English North America are purchased for work in the Jamestown settlement.

**1682**
René-Robert Cavelier, Sieur de La Salle, claims the Louisiana region for France.

**1700**

**1718**
Jean-Baptiste Bérnard de La Harpe establishes trading posts along the Red River.

Louisiana Territory map

**1759**
The Wichitas and Comanches defeat Colonel Diego Ortiz Parrilla's Spanish army at the Native Americans' fort on the Red River.

**1787**
The U.S. Constitution is written.

**1800**

**1803**
The Louisiana Purchase almost doubles the size of the United States.

**1803**
France sells the Louisiana Territory to the United States in the Louisiana Purchase.

## U.S. Events

**1830**

President Andrew Jackson signs the Indian Removal Act creating Indian Territory.

**1846–48**

The United States fights a war with Mexico over western territories in the Mexican War.

Oklahoma land rush, 1889

**1866**

Apache leader Geronimo surrenders to the U.S. Army, ending the last major Native American rebellion against the expansion of the United States into the West.

**1898**

The United States gains control of Cuba, Puerto Rico, the Philippines, and Guam after defeating Spain in the Spanish-American War.

**1917–18**

The United States engages in World War I.

**1920**

The Nineteenth Amendment to the U.S. Constitution grants women the right to vote.

## Oklahoma Events

**1830**

Native Americans from the East Coast travel westward into Oklahoma Territory in what is known as the Trail of Tears.

**1861**

Creek chief Opothle Yahola offers freedom to all Native Americans and African Americans who join him in a march to Kansas to fight the Confederacy.

**1862**

Congress passes the Homestead Act.

**1865–1886**

Cattle drives move through Indian Territory.

**1889**

The first official land run takes place.

**1896**

The first commercial oil well in Oklahoma is drilled.

**1900**

**1901**

The great land lottery opens the Kiowa, Comanche, Apache, and Wichita reservations to white settlement.

**1907**

Oklahoma becomes the 46th state.

**1921**

A race riot erupts in the city of Tulsa.

## U.S. Events

### 1929

The stock market crashes, plunging the United States more deeply into the Great Depression.

### 1941–45

The United States fights in World War II.

### 1964–73

The United States engages in the Vietnam War.

Oklahoma City National Memorial

### 2001

Terrorists hijack four U.S. aircraft and crash them into the World Trade Center in New York City, the Pentagon in Washington, D.C., and a Pennsylvania field, killing thousands.

### 2003

The United States and coalition forces invade Iraq.

## Oklahoma Events

### 1930s

The Dust Bowl devastates the plains.

Displaced Oklahomans during the Dust Bowl

### 1970

The McClellan-Kerr Arkansas River Navigation System is completed.

### 1995

The Murrah Federal Building in Oklahoma City is bombed.

### 1999

Dozens of tornadoes sweep the state, causing billions of dollars in damage.

**2000**

### 2013

A tornado strikes Moore, killing 24 people and injuring hundreds more.

# GLOSSARY

★ ★ ★

**biofuel** an energy source made from plants or plant-derived materials

**bogs** areas of wet, spongy ground

**buttes** narrow, flat-topped hills with very steep sides; types of mesas

**decathlon** an athletic contest of ten different track-and-field events

**derricks** towers that appear over oil wells

**desperadoes** bold or violent criminals, usually in the 19th-century western United States

**diaspora** the movement and scattering of people away from their homeland

**exodus** a mass departure from an area

**gypsum** a soft, white mineral

**heirlooms** items passed down, generally within a family, from generation to generation

**hydroelectric plants** facilities that use water power, typically through a dam, to produce electricity

**mesas** flat-topped hills

**nomadic** describing someone who moves from place to place and does not permanently settle in one location

**obsidian** jet-black volcanic glass

**pelts** animal skins covered in fur

**pentathlon** an athletic contest of five different track-and-field events

**plateau** an elevated part of the earth with steep slopes

**reservoir** a lake or tank for storing water

**segregated** set apart or separated from others by group or race

**sit-ins** acts of organized, nonviolent protest that involve sitting in a place and refusing to leave

# FAST FACTS

★ ★ ★

## State Symbols

| | |
|---|---|
| **Statehood date** | November 16, 1907, the 46th state |
| **Origin of state name** | Choctaw words meaning "red" and "people" |
| **State capital** | Oklahoma City |
| **State nickname** | The Sooner State |
| **State motto** | *Labor omnia vincit* ("Labor Conquers All Things") |
| **State bird** | Scissor-tailed flycatcher |
| **State flower** | Indian blanket |
| **State song** | "Oklahoma!" (see lyrics on page 128) |
| **State tree** | Redbud |
| **State stone** | Rose rock (barite rose) |
| **State fair** | Oklahoma City (mid-September) |

State seal

## Geography

| | |
|---|---|
| **Total area; rank** | 69,898 square miles (181,035 sq km); 20th |
| **Land; rank** | 68,667 square miles (177,848 sq km); 19th |
| **Water; rank** | 1,231 square miles (3,188 sq km); 30th |
| **Inland water; rank** | 1,231 square miles (3,188 sq km); 17th |
| **Geographic center** | 8 miles (13 km) north of Oklahoma City |
| **Latitude** | 33° 35' N to 37° N |
| **Longitude** | 94° 29' W to 103° W |
| **Highest point** | Black Mesa, 4,973 feet (1,516 m) |
| **Lowest point** | Little River, 289 feet (88 m), in McCurtain County |
| **Largest city** | Oklahoma City |
| **Number of counties** | 77 |
| **Longest river** | Two great river systems run through Oklahoma, the Red River (which forms a boundary with Texas) and the Arkansas |

State flag

# Population

| | |
|---|---|
| **Population; rank (2010 census)** | 3,751,351; 28th |
| **Density (2010 census)** | 55 persons per square mile (21 per sq km) |
| **Population distribution (2010 census)** | 66% urban, 34% rural |
| **Ethnic distribution (2010 census)** | White persons: 68.7% |
| | Black persons: 7.3% |
| | Asian persons: 1.7% |
| | American Indian and Alaska Native persons: 8.2% |
| | Native Hawaiian and Other Pacific Islander persons: 0.1% |
| | Persons reporting two or more races: 5.1% |
| | Hispanic or Latino persons: 8.9% |
| | People of some other race: 0.1% |

# Weather

| | |
|---|---|
| **Record high temperature** | 120°F (49°C) at Alva on July 18, 1936; at Altus on July 19 and August 12, 1936; and at Poteau on August 10, 1936 |
| **Record low temperature** | −31°F (−35°C) at Nowata on February 10, 2011 |
| **Average July temperature, Oklahoma City** | 83°F (28°C) |
| **Average January temperature, Oklahoma City** | 39°F (4°C) |
| **Average annual precipitation, Oklahoma City** | 36.5 inches (92.7 cm) |

# STATE SONG

★ ★ ★

## "Oklahoma!"

The song "Oklahoma," with words by Oscar Hammerstein II (1895–1960) and music by Richard Rodgers (1902–1979), was adopted by the Oklahoma legislature as the official state song on May 11, 1953.

Brand new state! Brand new state, gonna treat you great!
Gonna give you barley, carrots and pertaters,
Pasture fer the cattle, Spinach and Temayters!
Flowers on the prairie where the June bugs zoom,
Plen'y of air and plen'y of room,
Plen'y of room to swing a rope!
Plen'y of heart and plen'y of hope.

Oklahoma, where the wind comes sweepin' down the plain
And the wavin' wheat can sure smell sweet
When the wind comes right behind the rain.
Oklahoma, ev'ry night my honey lamb and I
Sit alone and talk and watch a hawk makin' lazy circles in the sky.
We know we belong to the land
And the land we belong to is grand!
And when we say—Yeow! A-yip-i-O-ee-ay!
We're only sayin' You're doin' fine, Oklahoma! Oklahoma—O.K.

# NATURAL AREAS AND HISTORIC SITES

★ ★ ★

## National Recreation Area

*Chickasaw National Recreation Area* includes 9,889 acres (4,002 ha) of rolling hills, forestland, and mineral springs, streams, and lakes.

*Winding Stair Mountain National Recreation Area* is located within the Ouachita National Forest near Talihina.

## National Historic Sites

*Washita Battlefield National Historic Site* commemorates a Southern Cheyenne village that was attacked by the U.S. Cavalry during the era of the Plains and Indian War.

## National Historic Trails

Sections of the *Trail of Tears National Historic Trail* and the *Santa Fe National Historic Trail* cross the state. The former is the route the Cherokee were forced to take when the government removed them from their homelands. The Santa Fe Trail was a route connecting Missouri in the east to Santa Fe in the west.

## National Memorial

*Oklahoma City National Memorial* honors the victims and survivors of the bombing at the site on April 19, 1995.

## National Forest

*Ouachita National Forest* is located near Talihina.

## National Grasslands

More than 30,000 acres (12,140 ha) of *Black Kettle and McClellan Creek National Grasslands* are in Oklahoma.

## State Parks

Oklahoma has 52 state parks and recreation areas. Lake Murray, Quartz Mountain, and Lake Wister state parks in the south, and Sequoyah State Park at Fort Gibson Reservoir, are among the most popular.

# SPORTS TEAMS

★ ★ ★

### NCAA Teams (Division I)

Oklahoma State University *Cowboys* and *Cowgirls*
Oral Roberts University *Golden Eagles*
University of Oklahoma *Sooners*
University of Tulsa *Golden Hurricanes*

# PROFESSIONAL SPORTS TEAMS

★ ★ ★

## National Basketball Association

Oklahoma City *Thunder*

The University of Oklahoma women's softball team

# CULTURAL INSTITUTIONS

★  ★  ★

### Libraries

The *Oklahoma Historical Society Library* (Oklahoma City) has a large collection on the state's history. Its mission is to preserve and perpetuate the history of Oklahoma and its people by collecting, interpreting, and disseminating knowledge of Oklahoma and the Southwest.

The *University of Oklahoma Library* (Norman) houses the DeGolyer collection on the history of science and technology, the Bass Business History collection, and the Western History Collections, an outstanding archive of Oklahoma and the American West.

### Museums

*Arbuckle Wilderness* (Davis) is an exotic animal park.

The *Oklahoma Historical Society Museum* at the Oklahoma History Center (Oklahoma City) is the largest museum in the state.

The *Oklahoma City National Memorial and Museum* (Oklahoma City) honors the victims, survivors, and rescuers of the bombing of the Murrah Federal Building in 1995.

*Philbrook Museum of Art* (Tulsa) has a noted collection of Native American arts and crafts.

The *Oklahoma WONDERtorium* (Stillwater) aims to entertain and educate children with a variety of different exhibits and programs.

*Cherokee Heritage Center* (Tahlequah) includes the Tsa-La-Gi Ancient Village, a re-creation of an Indian village. Cherokee Indians give tours during the summer months.

*Woolaroc Museum and Wildlife Preserve* (Bartlesville) displays some 55,000 historical artifacts.

### Performing Arts

*Oklahoma City Philharmonic* (Oklahoma City) has performed a diverse selection of music for the people of Oklahoma since 1988.

*Oklahoma City Ballet* (Oklahoma City) is a professional dance company that has performed works by some of the greatest choreographers of all time.

### Universities and Colleges

In 2011, Oklahoma had 17 public and 23 private institutions of higher learning.

# ANNUAL EVENTS

## January–April

**International Finals Rodeo** in Oklahoma City (January)

**Chocolate Festival** in Norman (February)

**An Affair of the Heart** in Oklahoma City (February)

**Azalea Festival** in Muskogee (April)

**Eighty-Niner Day Celebration** in Guthrie (April)

**Festival of the Arts** in Oklahoma City (April)

## May–August

**Fried Onion Burger Day Festival** in El Reno (May)

**Kolache Festival** in Prague (May)

**Red Earth Native American Festival** in Oklahoma City (May)

**Strawberry Festival** in Stilwell (second Saturday in May)

**Kiamichi Owa Chito Festival of the Forest** in Broken Bow (June)

**OK Mozart Festival** in Bartlesville (June)

**Pawnee Bill Wild West Show** in Pawnee (June)

**"Unto These Hills" outdoor drama** in Tahlequah (June–August)

**American Indian Exposition** in Anadarko (August)

**Rodeo and Old Cowhand Reunion** in Freedom (August)

## September–December

**Cherokee Strip Celebration** in Enid (September)

**Oklahoma State Fair** in Oklahoma City (September)

**Tulsa State Fair** in Tulsa (September–October)

**Robbers Cave Fall Festival** in Wilburton (October)

**Cheese Festival** in Watonga (October)

**Will Rogers Days** in Claremore (November)

**Territorial Christmas Celebration** in Guthrie (November–December)

# BIOGRAPHICAL DICTIONARY

**Troy Aikman (1966–)** is a television sports commentator and former NFL quarterback. He grew up in Henryetta and attended college at the University of Oklahoma.

**Chet Baker (1929–1988)** was a legendary jazz trumpter and singer. He was born in Yale.

**William Baker** See page 28.

**Louis Ballard (1931–2007)** was a composer who used Native American themes in his music. He was born in Miami.

**Johnny Bench (1947–)** is one of the most successful catchers in Major League Baseball history. Bench was baseball's Most Valuable Player in 1970 and 1972. He was born in Oklahoma City.

**John Berryman (1914–1972)** was a major figure in American poetry in the second half of the 20th century and was often considered one of the founders of the confessional school of poetry. He was born in McAlester.

**Garth Brooks (1962–)** is one of the most popular and best-selling country-western singers of all time. He was born in Tulsa.

**Jeremy Castle (1974–)** is a country-western singer and songwriter. He was born in Oklahoma City.

**Floyd Cooper (1959–)** is an award-winning children's book illustrator. He was born in Tulsa.

**Gordon Cooper (1927–2004)** was an astronaut who served on two missions: *Mercury 9* and *Gemini 5*. He was born in Shawnee.

**Francisco Vásquez de Coronado (1510–1554)** was a Spanish conquistador who made his way through what is now Oklahoma during Spain's early expeditions through North America.

**Angie Debo (1890–1988)** came to Oklahoma Territory as a child and became a writer and historian. In 1936, she wrote *And Still the Waters Run*, a book about the theft from Indians of their lands in Indian Territory.

**Ralph Ellison** See page 77.

**Mary Fallin** See page 90.

**Gloria Stewart Farley (1916–2006)** dedicated her life to searching for ancient rocks with hidden messages. Her main body of research was done on the Heavener Runestone in Oklahoma. She was born in Heavener.

Garth Brooks

John Hope Franklin

**John Hope Franklin (1915–2009)** was a historian who was born in Rentiesville and later lived in Tulsa. He is best known for the book *From Slavery to Freedom*. In 1995, he received the Presidential Medal of Freedom for his life's work.

**Tommy Franks (1945–)** was born in Waynewood. In June 2000, he was promoted to four-star general and assigned to be commander of the U.S. Central Command. Now retired, he received the Presidential Medal of Freedom in 2004, the nation's highest civilian award.

**James Garner (1928–)** is an American actor known primarily for his role as Jim Rockford in television's *The Rockford Files*. He was born in Norman.

**Raymond Gary (1908–1993)** was the governor of Oklahoma who helped end segregation in the state. He was born in Marshall County.

**Vince Gill (1957–)** is an award-winning country music singer. He was born in Norman.

**Sylvan Goldman** See page 102.

**Chester Gould (1900–1985)** was the cartoonist of the *Dick Tracy* comic strip. He was born in Pawnee.

**Blake Griffin** See page 81.

**Woody Guthrie** See page 59.

**Bill Hader (1978–)** is an actor and comedian who is best known as a cast member on Saturday Night Live. He was born and raised in Tulsa.

**LaDonna Harris (1931–)** is the founder and president of Americans for Indian Opportunity. She was born in Lawton.

**Paul Harvey (1918–2009)** was a radio commentator best known for his segments called *The Rest of the Story*. He was born in Tulsa.

**Tony Hillerman (1925–2008)** wrote best-selling mystery novels involving Navajo traditions. He was born in Sacred Heart.

Tony Hillerman

Ron Howard

**S. E. Hinton** See page 75.

**Ron Howard (1954–)** is an actor and director. He has starred in several television series and directed a number of movies, including *Apollo 13*. He was born in Duncan.

**Wanda Jackson (1937–)** is a country singer who is known as the Queen of Rockabilly. She was born in Maud and came to fame singing on an Oklahoma City radio show as a high school student.

**Karl Jansky (1905–1950)** was a scientist who founded radio astronomy. Today, the unit used to measure the strength of radio sources is called the jansky. He was born in Norman.

**Ben Johnson (1918–1996)** was a famous actor who starred mainly in Western films, usually playing ranchers and cowboys. He was born in Pawhuska.

**Jennifer Jones (1919–2009)** was an Academy Award– and Golden Globe–winning actress. She was born in Tulsa.

**William Wayne Keeler** See page 100.

**Jeane Jordan Kirkpatrick (1926–2006)** was the first woman to serve as the U.S. ambassador to the United Nations. She was born in Duncan.

**Shannon Lucid** See page 71.

**Wilma Mankiller (1945–2010)** was the principal chief of the Cherokee Nation for 10 years, the first woman to hold that office. Born in Stilwell, she got her name from a warrior ancestor.

Wilma Mankiller

**Mickey Mantle (1931–1995)** was one of the greatest baseball players of all time. He was born in Spavinaw and played for the New York Yankees. He was named Most Valuable Player three times and inducted into the Baseball Hall of Fame in 1974.

**Edwin P. McCabe** See page 47.

**Reba McEntire (1955–)** is a popular country-western singer who had her own television series. She was born in McAlester.

**Shannon Miller (1977–)** is an Olympic gymnast from Edmond. She has won more medals than any other American gymnast.

**Leona Mitchell (1949–)** is a well-known opera star. She was born in Enid.

**N. Scott Momaday (1934–)** won the Pulitzer Prize for fiction. The son of Kiowa Indians, he was born in Lawton.

**Bill Moyers (1934–)** is a journalist who has worked with PBS and CBS networks and has won more than 30 Emmys for his reports. He was born in Hugo.

**Olivia Munn (1980–)** is a model and actress who has appeared in a variety of movies and television shows. She was born in Oklahoma City.

**William Murray** See page 86.

**Lauren Nelson (1987–)** won the 2007 Miss America pageant, becoming the sixth woman from Oklahoma to win that title. She was born in Lawton.

**Steven Owens (1947–)** was the Heisman Trophy winner in 1969 and is the Oklahoma Sooners' all-time highest scorer with 55 touchdowns. He was born in Gore.

**Patti Page (1927–2013)** was one of the best-known American pop music singers of the 20th century. She was born in Claremore.

**Frank Phillips** See page 54.

**Bill Pickett** See page 44.

**Brad Pitt (1963–)** is an actor, known for his roles in movies such as *Twelve Monkeys* and *Ocean's Eleven*. He was born in Shawnee.

Olivia Munn

**Tony Randall (1920–2004)** was a comedic actor who starred in the TV show *The Odd Couple*. He was born in Tulsa.

**Will Rogers** See page 78.

**Blake Shelton (1976–)** is a country singer and songwriter and a judge on popular television show *The Voice*. He was born and raised in Ada, Oklahoma.

**James A. "Jim" Shoulders (1928–2007)** has won more World Championship Rodeo Cowboy awards than any other Professional Rodeo Cowboys Association contestant. He was born in Oiltown.

**Billy Sims (1955–)** won the Heisman Trophy in 1978 as an Oklahoma Sooner. He led the Sooners to two consecutive Orange Bowl titles in three straight appearances.

**Thomas Stafford (1930–)** is an astronaut who has been on four space missions. He was born in Weatherford.

**Willie Stargell (1940–2001)** was a professional baseball player from Earlsboro. He was elected to the Baseball Hall of Fame in 1988 and helped his team win the World Series in 1971 and 1979.

Brad Pitt

Marjorie Tallchief (left)

**Elizabeth Warren (1949–)** was elected a U.S. senator from Massachusetts in 2013. She was born in Oklahoma City and grew up in Norman.

**Cornel West (1953–)** is a philosopher, scholar, and political activist. he was born in Tulsa.

**Charlie Wilson (1953–)** is a musician who came to fame in the 1970s as the lead singer of the Gap Band and later established a successful solo career. He was born and raised in Tulsa.

**Maria Tallchief (1925–2013)** and **Marjorie Tallchief (1927–)** were professional ballerinas. These sisters, members of the Osage Nation, were born in Fairfax.

**Joyce Carol Thomas (1938–)** is the author of more than 50 books for children. She writes poems, plays, and books, many of which center on the culture and history of Oklahoma. She was born in Ponca City.

**Jim Thorpe** See page 80.

**Carrie Underwood (1983–)** is an award-winning pop country singer who gained fame by winning the *American Idol* title in 2005. She was born in Muskogee and raised on a farm in Checotah.

**Billy Vessels (1931–2001)** was the Heisman Trophy winner in 1952. He went on to play for the Baltimore Colts after being the second overall pick in the NFL draft in 1953. He was born in Cleveland.

**Sam Walton (1918–1992)** was a businessman who founded the Wal-Mart and Sam's Club retail chains. He was born in Kingfisher.

Carrie Underwood

# RESOURCES

★ ★ ★

## BOOKS

### Nonfiction

Frisch, Aaron. *Oklahoma City Thunder*. Mankato, MN: Creative Education, 2012.

McNeese, Tim. *The Louisiana Purchase: Growth of a Nation*. New York: Chelsea House, 2009.

Reis, Ronald A. *Mickey Mantle*. New York: Chelsea House, 2008.

Rhynes, Martha E. *Ralph Ellison: Author of Invisible Man*. Greensboro, NC: Morgan Reynolds, 2006.

Saylor-Marchant, Linda. *Oklahoma*. New York: Children's Press, 2009.

Zuchora-Walske, Christine. *The Dust Bowl*. Ann Arbor, MI: Cherry Lake Publishing, 2014.

### Fiction

Antle, Nancy. *Beautiful Land: A Story of the Oklahoma Land Rush* (Once Upon America). New York: Puffin Publishing, 1997.

Beard, Darleen Bailey. *The Babbs Switch Story*. New York: Farrar, Straus and Giroux, 2002.

Hesse, Karen. *Out of the Dust*. New York: Scholastic, 1997.

McCaughrean, Geraldine. *Stop the Train!* New York: HarperTrophy, 2005.

Rawls, Wilson. *Summer of the Monkeys*. New York: Yearling, 1998.

Rawls, Wilson. *Where the Red Fern Grows*. New York: Yearling, 1996.

Visit this Scholastic Web site for more information on Oklahoma:
**www.factsfornow.scholastic.com**
Enter the keyword **Oklahoma**

# AUTHOR'S TIPS AND SOURCE NOTES

★　　★　　★

My first awareness of Oklahoma came when I was young. As a huge fan of musical theater, I knew the play *Oklahoma* quite well and could sing along with almost every song in it. I even figured out what "a surrey with the fringe on top" meant.

To discover more about this state, I read a lot of books and spent many hours online. I studied the history of the state and was particularly struck by the lifestyles of the Native Americans of Oklahoma.

I read a number of great nonfiction books about the state, but it was the fiction books that often gave me a real sense of Oklahoma lives throughout history. For example, *The Journal of C. J. Jackson, a Dust Bowl Migrant, Oklahoma to California, 1935* by William Durbin (Scholastic, 2002) put the facts and figures I knew into perspective. I learned more about the tribal cultures in *Spirits Dark and Light: Supernatural Tales from the Five Civilized Tribes* by Tim Tingle (August House, 2006). Of course, just talking to the people of Oklahoma was one of the best sources for what life in their state is like!